VIJAY GUPTA, M.D., is a practicing physician and sonologist in Jaipur. Attracted by the stock market, he suffered some early losses. He then did intensive research on investing and trading methods which eventually led him to create the mechanical trading system revealed in this book. His main focus has been to develop methods which are not only based on well established principles of technical analysis but which can be proven by an unbiased analysis of historical data. Dr. Gupta also believes that it is impossible for a trader to succeed without strict rules of money management. His trading experience over the last two decades has also made him realize that lack of discipline in pursuing one's own proven strategies is the single most important reason why traders fail. His trading philosophy can be summarized as follows:

Trade with the trend
Cut your losses short
Let the profits run
Manage your money well.

Dr. Gupta is now an active trader of stocks and commodity futures, alongside his medical practice.

HOW I MAKE MONEY IN TRADING *and* How You Can, *Too!*

VIJAY GUPTA

www.visionbooksindia.com

www.visionbooksindia.com

Disclaimer

The author and the publisher disclaim all legal or other responsibilities for any losses which investors may suffer by investing or trading using the methods described in this book. Readers are advised to seek professional guidance before making any specific investments.

A Vision Books Original

First Published 2019
Reprinted 2019, 2023

ISBN 10: 93-86268-29-9
ISBN 13: 978-93-86268-29-7

Published by
Vision Books Pvt. Ltd.
(Incorporating Orient Paperbacks and CARING imprints)
24 Feroze Gandhi Road, Lajpat Nagar 3
New Delhi-110024, India.
Phone: (+91-11) 2984 0821 / 22
e-mail: visionbooks@gmail.com

Printed at
Ashim Print Line
38/2, 35 & 36 Sahibabad Industrial Area, Ghaziabad
Uttar Pradesh 201010, India.

Contents

Part 2
~
The Essentials of Trading

Acknowledgments

I was inspired to learn and use technical analysis by a book I read in 2001, *The Psychology of Technical Analysis* written by Tony Plummer and published in India by Vision Books. Both the author and the publisher deserve my whole-hearted thanks.

I thank Tony Plummer for having written the only book which provides an answer to the question as to why technical analysis works. Without first knowing the answer to this why, I could never have progressed to the point of trading successfully using technical analysis. Tony Plummer's book not only gave me a full-fledged system to start my trading career but also opened my mind to totally new ways of thinking which fulfilled my life in many other ways.

I thank Vision Books for having had the courage to bring high quality trading books from across the world into our country at attractively low prices without which I may not have been prompted to buy books by such great authors as Tony Plummer, Edward and Maggie, Martin Pring, Cynthia Case, Prof. Edelson, etc., nor acquire whatever knowledge that I have today.

I had planned to write this book many years ago. I couldn't take out the time to do so due to my busy medical practice as well as passion for trading. It was only when my daughter Tanya and my son Kanav freed me from the day to day management of trading that I was able to start devoting a little time for putting my knowledge into the written word. Not only that; their involvement improved my trading profits substantially. They did not take much time to understand that discipline is the most important component of success in trading. All my affection goes to them.

My wife, Mamta, has always been a pillar of support for me. She not only tolerated my isolation but also my periodic irritable behavior. She provided me great company while I learnt technical analysis and due to her almost equal knowledge, she offered many suggestions which have helped to make this book a better one. My thanks to her cannot be fully expressed in words.

I also thank Shri M. K. Gupta, my friend and a very intelligent and experienced stock analyst, who read the manuscript of the book with a critic's eye and offered invaluable suggestions.

My special thanks go to those who knew that I was "doing something" while learning technical analysis, but were always skeptical about its usefulness. It was partly due to their unwavering skepticism that I was motivated to make myself a successful trader and technical analyst!

My sincere thanks go to the editorial staff at Vision Books whose inputs have helped to tremendously improve the book.

~

Preface

Must every technical analyst or successful trader write a book? Since every trader who has made money from trading somehow feels compelled to talk about his success story, there is every reason that a book should not be written only because of that. One of the most renowned technical analysts, Tony Plummer, remarked while reviewing Cynthia Case's book *Trading With the Odds*:

> "There are three things that should be expected from a new book on investment — original ideas, a rigorous philosophical framework, and a coherent presentation."

I certainly do not intend to write an investment bible nor is it my aim to simply rewrite the familiar in my own way. I believe that you will find new ideas in this book which are not only aimed at providing the reader with solutions to some existing problems but also a framework by which he can lay the foundation of his trading career. The book will, hopefully, meet Tony Plummer's criteria.

The book, however, is intended more as a practical guide than a comprehensive treatise on technical analysis and trading. There are a lot of excellent treatises on both these subjects and I do not feel that there is any need for another.

~

I am a physician by profession and got attracted to seeking out analytical methods after my early failures in trading and investing. It is true that most investors start out as fundamentalists and later turn to technical analysis due to the need for better timing of entries and exits. Certainly, my own experience has been that.

Being a student of science, I was not satisfied with methods which required substantial subjective inputs. Although highly impressed by the Elliot Wave Theory and traditional technical analysis, I found it difficult to put these into practice. This may have been due to my lack of understanding but it's also a fact that the Elliot Wave count is something about which no two traders are ever in agreement!

The dilemma for me was clear. Should I try to make a reasonable profit on a consistent and predictable basis, or should I wait for opportunities which could give me large profits — or perhaps a large loss? Mind you, trying to make even small profits consistently is not as easy as it sounds. A thorough knowledge of the subject is required and one's quest is always to find a simple, yet effective, approach.

Mechanical methods can be developed and can fulfill this need quite well, but as a trader I quickly realized that it is not possible to succeed without discipline and adherence to strict money management rules. Discipline is the more formidable challenge here because prices are always moving in favor or against one's trading position and, either way, they instill fear in one's mind. A mechanical strategy, proven over a long period, then gets interfered with and the plan of making consistent, small profits comes to a standstill.

The presence and role of fear in the financial markets should never be taken lightly. Fear does not entirely go away even after sufficient experience because the responses generated by fear are too deep-rooted to be eradicated merely by a few years of experience.

One needs to be bold and show courage in times of adversity. There is also the need for an analysis of specific factors which trigger the fear response. Such factors are usually completely unrelated to the trading system being used and are unwarranted extraneous inputs. For example, a trading position which has been established due to a signal from your trading system should not be exited merely because of some other analyst's contrary opinion on a television channel. The extraneous input may not always be so obvious, it can even be very subtle. For example, suppose the trading system in use requires that the long position be exited only when a significant low has been broken on the chart. The trader, however, notices a sell signal on a moving average crossover and exits his long position due to this crossover. If acting on such a crossover was not a part of his original, well researched plan, then the trader would find, to his dismay, that he had exited his long position prematurely. A trader must keep working diligently towards eliminating all such extraneous factors from his or her mind.

~

Part 1

~

Stock Markets

Know Your Battleground

1
~
Secrets of the Stock Market

"The fact is that the markets do not have any secrets to hide"

The stock market is a platform for the buying and selling of stocks at prices which are determined by market participants. Since fear is the most prevalent sentiment in stock markets, traders are always looking for something which may help them overcome their fear. Although the causes of fear are altogether different from what one may be inclined to think, the feeling that they are not privy to secrets of the stock market serves to enhance the fears of market participants. The fact is that the stock market does not have any secrets to hide. Lack of sufficient knowledge, lack of requisite capital and lack of discipline are the root causes of failure in the stock markets and repeated failures make market participants wonder about the secrets of the markets when actually they should be thinking about the sufficiency, or otherwise, of their own knowledge.

Thus, instead of looking for non-existent secrets, it would be better for traders and investors to understand the true reality and nature of the markets.

Markets are Volatile and Mean Reverting

One permanent feature of the stock market is that it always keeps on fluctuating up and down. These seemingly random up and down movement happens around a mean. Furthermore, the movements can be seen in all time frames, be it weekly, daily, hourly, or even every minute. Most traders make the mistake of considering the market as volatile if the market doesn't behave "properly," i.e. the prices do not go in the direction s/he wants. However, this is not true as the markets are always having a certain degree of volatility which can be measured using mathematical formulas. In the sense in which this term is commonly used, we may notice that what seems a nicely uptrending market on weekly charts is full of up and down movements on shorter time frame charts. In such a case, while the long term investors are enjoying their notional gains, a trader looking at weekly charts is left wondering as to how to make a profit. He would have preferred the market to undergo a correction and provide him with an opportunity of a low risk entry. He must analyze smaller time frame charts to accomplish his goal. Let me explain this with the help of an example (*see* Figure 1.1).

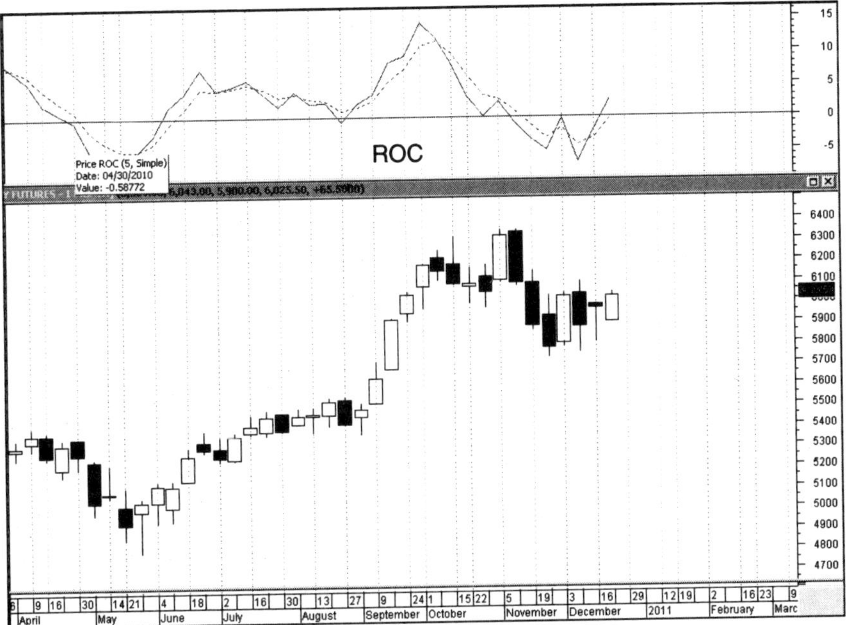

Figure 1.1: **This weekly chart of Nifty futures doesn't reveal even a single low risk trading opportunity to go long even though Nifty rose significantly in this period**

~

Based on the trading system described in this book, the weekly chart of Nifty futures in Figure 1.1, for example, didn't reveal even a single low risk opportunity of going long between May to December 2010 even though there is evidence of a significant advance in prices. The trend seemed to have turned up somewhere in May / June and the trader would have needed some evidence of a correction to take a long position but there was none till November, by which time most of the gains would already have been made by those having a system to enter at lower levels. Traders looking at daily or hourly charts, however, would have been provided decent low risk trading opportunities as shown in figures 1.2 and 1.3.

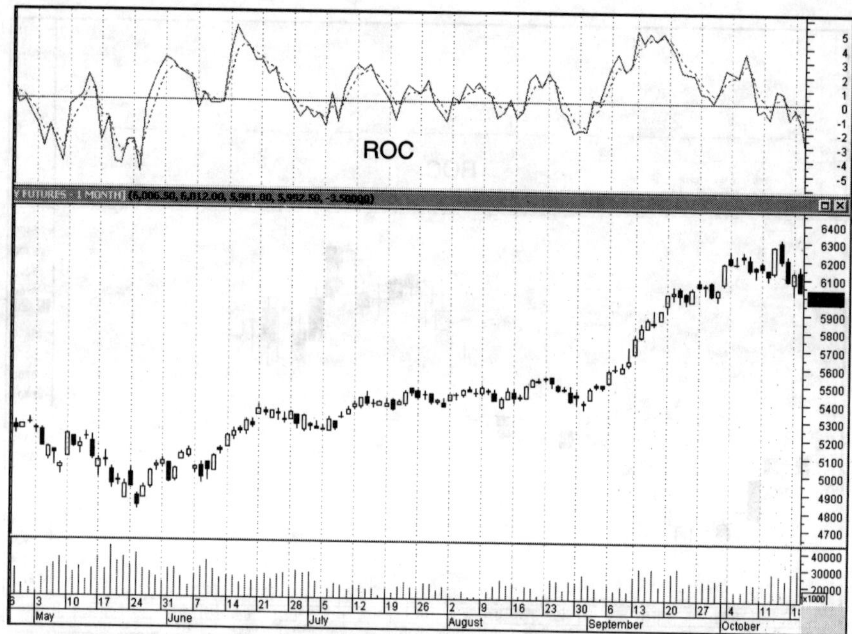

Figure 1.2: **The daily chart of Nifty, for a part of the time period shown in Figure 1.1, throws up several opportunities when low risk entries into long positions could have been made. The upper part of the chart shows that there were many occasions when the ROC-based mechanical swing, as described later in the book, gave profitable buy signals.**

~

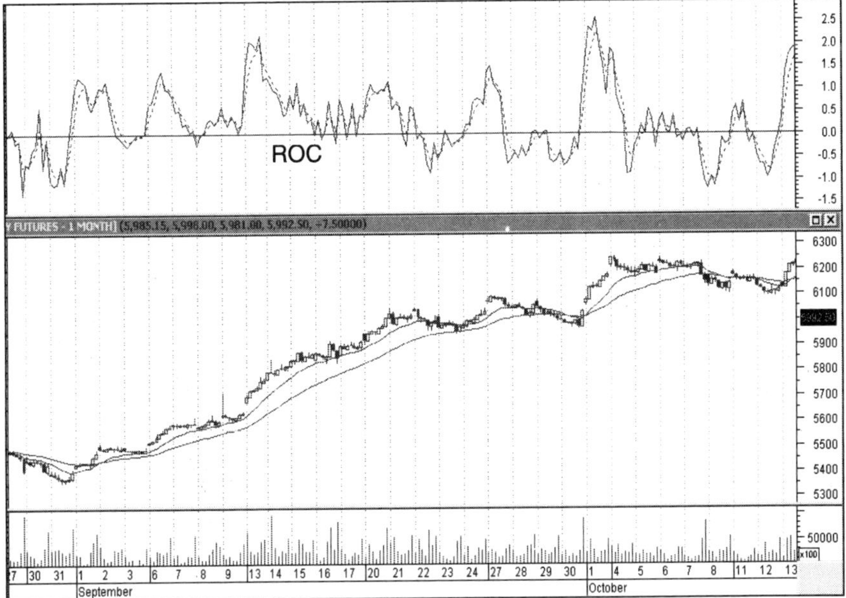

Figure 1.3: **The hourly chart of Nifty futures for — a part of the period covered in Figure 1.1 and Figure 1.2 — throws up multiple opportunities for entry into long positions on the basis of the ROC-based mechanical swing method discussed in this book.**

~

The volatility of the market, evident in all time frames, whether charted hourly, daily, or weekly, is what enables traders to find profitable opportunities. Traders, and equally investors, have to understand the fact that any profits that they make from the stock market are dependent upon the fact that markets are volatile, i.e. they move up and down. Clearly, then, traders should not blame the market for making a move against their trading position, nor waste time in pondering why the market is making an adverse move. Rather, they should focus their attention on preserving their capital at such junctures, and stick to whatever exit strategy they have already planned at the time of entry.

It is also, however, a fact that such up and down movements occur alternatively and during the process the price either crosses its mean on the upside or on the downside. In other words, prices overshoot the mean. For example, a 200-day moving average (200DMA) is usually regarded as a good indicator of the market's long term direction and may be considered as the "mean" for the purpose of our discussion. This average is shown in Figure 1.4. The mean reverting feature of the markets should caution the traders that they should not become either too bullish or too bearish when the market is over extended on any one side. Instead, they should focus on booking profits at such times.

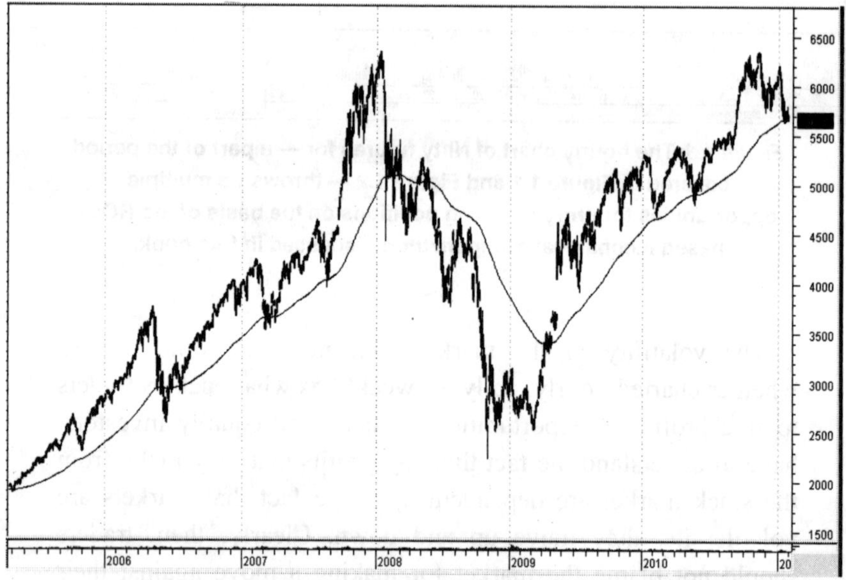

Figure 1.4: **Daily chart of Nifty with a 200-day moving average line**

~

Are Markets Irresponsible?

Dramatic figures are often flaunted to showcase that the stock markets have given such and such returns over such and such a period. These returns appear fantastic. It is also widely publicized, or implied, that such high returns will continue to occur in the future as well. While this may be true over a long period of time, market behavior can often be baffling not only in the short term but, sometimes, also in long term when the market seemingly starts behaving "irresponsibly" and the expected gains do not materialize. For example, the Japanese stock market witnessed a bear market from 1990 to 2017. It started to rise thereafter but even in 2017, its index, the Nikkei, was still at half of its level as compared to the peak of 1990, i.e. even after a period of approximately 27 years. The US market (Dow Jones Index) was trading near the same level in December 2010 as it had been in January 2000, while Nasdaq was trading at less than half its value of March 2000 ten years later (*see* Figures 1.5 and 1.6).

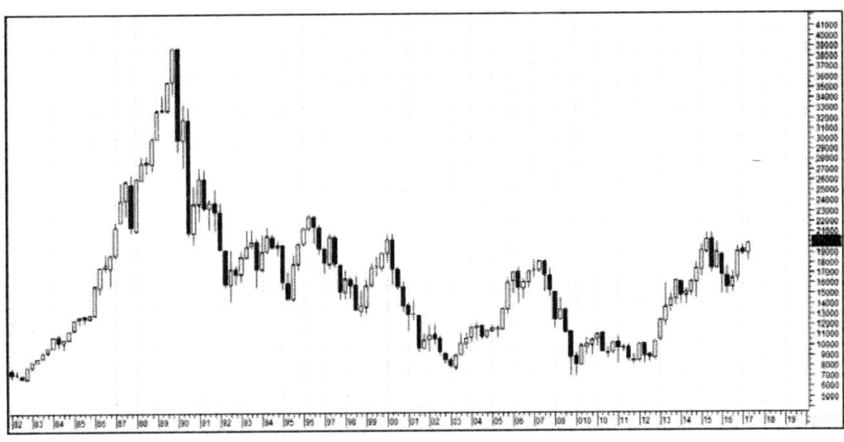

Figure 1.5: **Quarterly chart of Nikkei from 1982 to 2017. An endless bear market?**

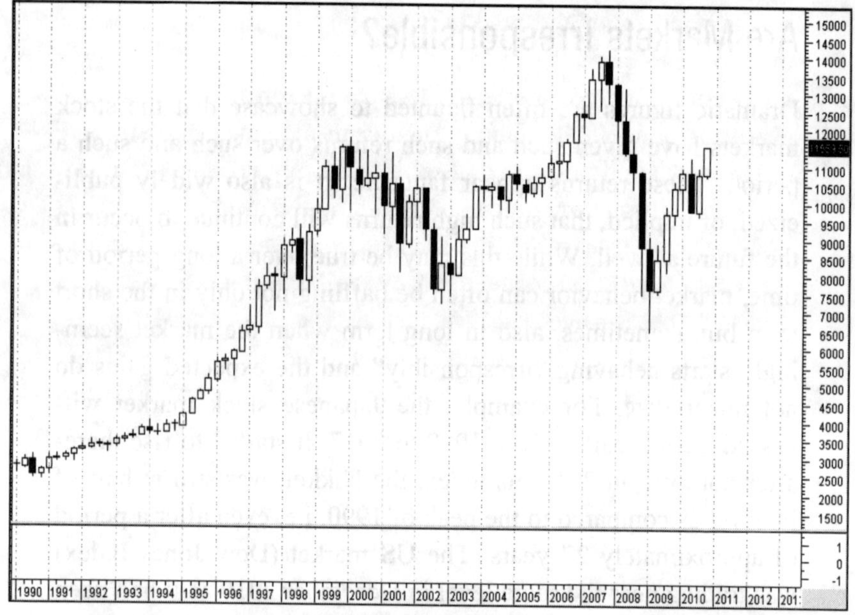

Figure 1.6: **Quarterly chart of the Dow Jones index. In 2010, the index was still trading at approximately the same level as in March 2000.**

~

You can't therefore depend upon the market to provide any pre-defined returns to you. Instead, devote all your energies to developing strategies which will help you survive and make money, whatever course the market may chart in future.

Markets are Not for the Ignorant

Though a small trader has some advantages when it comes to fast entries and exits, in general, however, the market treats an ignorant small trader in the same way as a new customer is treated by a shopkeeper. The shopkeeper wants to make a sale to the new customer even if a few lies have to be spoken in the process. Similarly, seasoned market players have to offload their stock to someone, and who can be better for this purpose other than a gullible small investor or trader? An individual investor often does not have the resources to research his position diligently, is quite excited about playing in the stock market (as if this were a good past time!), and is generally dependent on second-hand information doled out to him by the media.

Actually, an individual trader should not consider himself disadvantaged due to the small capital at his disposal. But if his knowledge regarding the stock market is limited, then he is indeed vulnerable.

Once you have the right strategy in place and are determined to succeed in the market, the market provides you a level playing field and you do not have to worry about any cartels or operators diminishing your chances. After all, these cartels cannot operate in complete secrecy because every transaction of shares has to take place through the exchange and is, therefore, knowable to market participants. Once you have acquired the requisite knowledge, you will more often be on the side of the cartels, rather than running against them.

Impact of Insiders on the Markets

Despite all the regulations in place, there is no denying that both insider news and buying and selling by insiders have a large impact on particular stock prices even though the market as a whole is rarely affected by this. Insider news, however, is more likely to have a strong impact on thinly traded stocks. It is unlikely to significantly impact the fifty stocks that form the Nifty index for example, but can have more pronounced impact on small cap stocks and, sometimes, in mid cap stocks as well. So, it's a good idea to keep away from small cap and mid cap stocks until you have better understood how the market behaves. Furthermore, even if you get an inside tip on some stock, do not establish a position in it without doing your own independent research as well.

You won't have to worry about these issues once you finish reading this book since the purpose of this book is to provide you with strategies which are not only proven but are also not dependent on dubious, and often illegal, means of making money in the market.

It is safe to say that if you are trading in larger capitalized, highly liquid stocks then you can generally ignore the existence and actions of market insiders.

The Dow Theory is Essentially Correct

Dow Theory and Elliot Wave Theory describe the nature of market movements and are essentially correct. **These theories, however, should not be depended upon for making predictions.** A trader should initiate a trade only on the basis of a well thought out strategy he is comfortable with, and then manage the trade diligently, with an eye on profits and preservation of capital at all times. One should not stick to any pre-defined profit targets lest these distract your attention from the final exit strategy. The only prudent use of targets is to tighten the stop loss whenever the price nears your target.

Although these theories help us to define price patterns amidst what seems like utter chaos, and thus appear able to help us formulate profitable strategies, their subjective nature makes it rather difficult to generate superior returns in comparison with simple mechanical strategies.

The Markets Discount Everything

This is the most important characteristic of financial markets and an understanding of this phenomenon can lead to handsome profits. The proponents of efficient market hypothesis (EMH) emphatically remind us that if there is any news or event which may have an effect on the fortunes of a company, the price of that company's stock will immediately get readjusted to reflect that impact. Hence, any opportunity to profit from such knowledge can only be extremely short lived.

But what they forget is that even this process of discounting can have an emotional element in it. If the market participants were completely rational, then there wouldn't be any markets as we know them. Yet, there are prolonged bull markets and also prolonged bear markets. It is well known that valuations are overly stretched at the height of a bull market and the same valuations then become extremely attractive (low) in the bear market that follows. If the price were discounting everything in a rational manner, then there would be no occasion for under- or

> **The Efficient Market Hypothesis** (EMH) is an investment theory which holds that share prices reflect all available information and consistent positive returns are therefore impossible. It follows then that neither technical nor fundamental analysis can produce excess risk adjusted returns and only inside information can result in outsized risk adjusted returns. According to EMH, stocks always trade at their fair value on stock exchanges, making it impossible for investors to either purchase undervalued stocks or sell stocks at inflated prices. As such, it should be impossible to outperform the overall market through expert stock selection or market timing, and the only way an investor can possibly obtain higher returns is by purchasing riskier investments.

over-valuation? After a long tug-of-war, the participants will agree that this is the fair price of XYZ stock after taking into consideration all previously existing information regarding the stock. The price should then not change unless a new event takes place. But the price has this funny habit of continuously changing. Even without any "reason!"

Not everybody who has a stake in Company XYZ is participating every minute the market is open. There are promoters who do not even bother about day-to-day price moves in their company's stock. Then there are the long term investors who simply do not feel the need to track news related to the company they are invested in. Finally, when all the current participants have agreed on a fair price, someone comes along with a large holding and who is in such dire need of money that he is willing to sell at whatever price he can. The price will adjust to such a large sell order by going down. But is this an event related to the company? Or, is it simply an absence of a large buyer at that time? Be that as it may, in the process an opportunity has been provided to those who are tracking and trading the stock.

The trading strategy given in this book is designed for taking advantage of times when the discounting process gets derailed, and there is overwhelming market evidence that this happens more frequently than the proponents of efficient market hypothesis will care to admit.

Trending Markets *versus* Sideways Markets

When markets make a sustained move in any one direction, whether up or down, they are said to be trending. An uptrending market is usually called a bull market, while a downtrending market is usually called a bear market. When markets are trading in a range, they are said to be sideways.

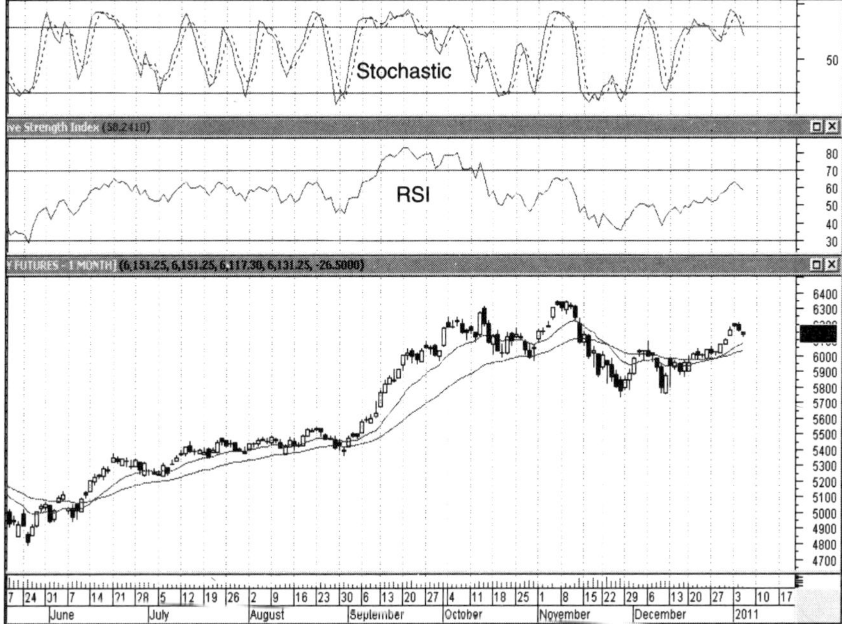

Figure 1.7: **Daily chart of Nifty futures shows moving averages, RSI and stochastic oscillator.**

~

Trading systems which are designed for use in one type of market may give losses if used in the other type. For example, moving average crossover systems often give excellent profits in trending markets result in huge draw downs, i.e. losses, in sideways markets. On the other hand, oscillators or momentum indicators are generally used for trading in sideway markets. Indicators such as Rate of Change (ROC), Stochastic Oscillator or Relative Strength Index (RSI) are used to define overbought or oversold condition of the market (*see* Figure 1.7). If the market is oversold, a long position is established while if the market is overbought, the long position is exited and a short position is established.

Most of the momentum indicators provide similar information and, ideally, only any one of them should be part of a good system otherwise there is danger of information overload and resultant confusion.

How can a trader decide which type of market he is in? Wells Wilder, an excellent trader and developer of many indicators, including the famous RSI, developed Directional Movement Indicator (ADX) for this purpose (*see* Figure 1.8). When ADX value rises above the level of 25, the market is said to be trending either up or down. The direction of trend has to be gauged from the price chart. For a detailed discussion on this indicator,

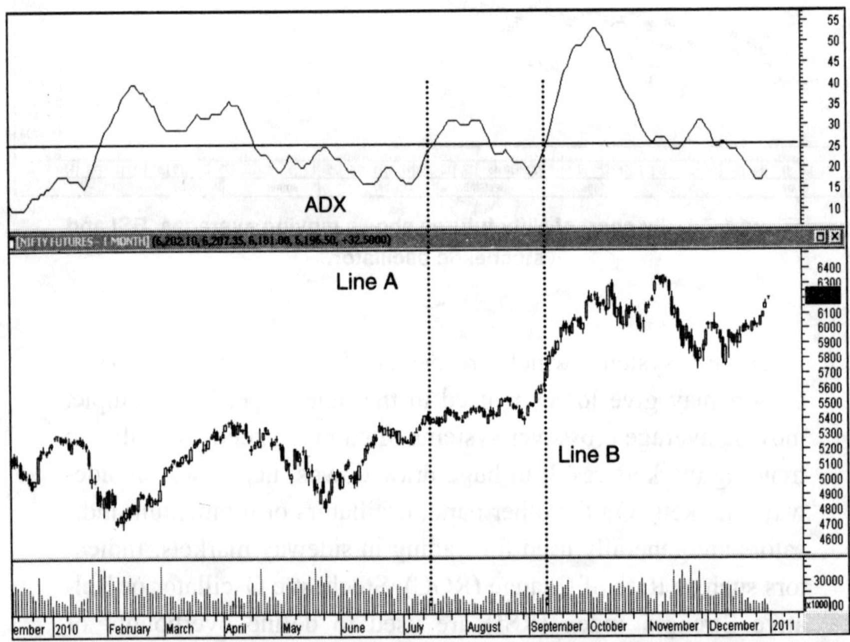

Figure 1.8: **Daily chart of Nifty futures showing the 14-period ADX in the upper panel. Line A and Line B show the points when ADX went above 25. On both these occasions, the prices had already advanced quite significantly.**

~

the reader should refer to *Martin Pring on Market Momentum*. But as a trader of several years' experience, I have not found this tool to provide any extra advantage, insofar as the system which I use and which is being described in this book is concerned. The problem is not with the concept of ADX but with the purpose of including it in a trading system. If the system is already using some sort of trend indicator (moving averages or trend lines, etc.) then adding ADX will only result in confusion.

I propose a simpler definition of trending and sideway markets for trading purposes: when the chart of time frame being traded — say, daily — and the chart of one degree higher time frame — say, weekly — are both showing an uptrend, the markets should be considered bullish and trending — and *vice versa*.

If, on the other hand, the trend in the daily time frame is down but that in the next higher degree (weekly) time frame chart is up, the market should be considered as bullish and sideways. By this logic, a trader can have four possible scenarios as summarised in Table 1.1.

Table 1.1

Trend in Chart of Time Frame Being Traded	*Trend in Chart of Higher Time Frame*	*Market Trend*
Uptrend	Uptrend	Bullish and trending
Downtrend	Uptrend	Bullish and sideways
Downtrend	Downtrend	Bearish and trending
Uptrend	Downtrend	Bearish and sideways

It is much easier to make money during trends than during sideways markets. Hence, the main focus of a trader should always be to ride the big trends from the earliest possible moment to the last moment and the trading system should be designed in such a manner that most, if not all, of the big trades are taken advantage of. The system revealed in this book is one such system.

Let us elaborate on this a bit more.

When the weekly chart is showing an uptrend, a trader needs to wait for a correction to enter the trend. Even though such a correction may not be obvious on the weekly chart, it will be quite evident on the daily chart. While the trend is still up on the weekly chart, it will be seen as being down on the daily chart.

A trader trading in the daily timeframe now has two choices. He may buy the oversold conditions and sell the overbought conditions (range trader) or he may buy on a swing breakout (trend trader). The trend trader will go long if the markets are bullish and trending, or when the markets are bullish and sideways but will not take a long position when the markets are bearish and trending, or when the markets are bearish and sideways. Correspondingly, a trend trader will go short if the markets are bearish and trending or when the markets are bearish and sideways but will not take a short position when the markets are either bullish and trending or when the markets are bullish and sideways.

A range trader, on the other hand, will go long as well as short when the markets are bullish and sideways or when the markets are bearish and sideways but will keep away from the markets when they are either bullish and trending or when they are bearish and trending. This does not, however, mean that a trader cannot trade both types (trending and sideways) of markets but that will require him to be quite nimble.

~

2

~

Fundamental Analysis *versus* Technical Analysis

Fundamental analysis requires an analysis of data related to a company or market and then reaching a conclusion whether to buy or sell at the prevailing price or not, depending upon the fair value arrived at by the analysis. The data studied may be price to earning (PE) ratio, price to book value (PBV) ratio, sales growth, dividend yield, cash flow, etc. Importance is also placed on the quality of management and the company's competitive abilities. All of these factors, and some more, may be assigned different weightage to arrive at a "fair value" of its stock.

Technical analysis, on the other hand, is simply an analysis of the supply and demand mismatch based on market generated data, such as price, volume, open interest, etc. Nowadays, software is easily and widely available for graphic representation of these data. Several types of mathematical indicators can be applied and conclusions can then be drawn as to specific entry points, stop losses, etc. Although prediction is not a necessary part of technical analysis, as opposed to fundamental analysis, it is possible to estimate probabilistic future price targets as well.

Fundamental Analysis

In an excellent discussion on the subject, Jake Bernstein in his book *Profits in the Futures Markets* has summarized the shortcomings of fundamental analysis:

1. Not all fundamentals can be known at any given time.
2. The importance of different fundamentals varies at different times.
3. The average speculator may have difficulty gathering and interpreting the wealth of information that is available for every market.
4. Fundamental analysis often fails to answer the important question that faces most speculators — the question of timing.
5. Many fundamental statistics are available only after the fact.
6. Fundamentals can be significantly altered by abrupt changes in weather, politics, international events, and economic policies.
7. The effort required in gathering, updating, and interpreting fundamental data may not, in the long run, yield efficient results.
8. Fundamental analysis does not provide alternatives based on price action, but rather on changes in underlying conditions.

Fundamental analysis is more useful for long term investment strategies and for investors with a high risk appetite. The ultimate purpose of fundamental analysis is to find a stock with adequate "margin of safety," i.e. to buy the stock when it seems to be undervalued as compared to the assets owned by the company. This is supposed to limit the downside risk. This approach, however, which is known more commonly as "bottom up investing," is not foolproof since an undervalued stock may continue to lose even more value due to macro-economic factors, such as interest rates and GDP. A study of macro-economic factors which may have an influence on stock prices is known as "top down investing." Sophisticated investors like Warren Buffett combine both the approaches. They will not buy an undervalued stock if macro-economic factors do not favor such a move; nor will they buy an over-valued stock just because the macro-economic factors are favorable.

Technical Analysis

The only data required for technical analysis is price — volume and open interest may be useful as confirmatory data but are not essential for technical analysis. Thus, the trader always has first rate data as soon as they are being generated and is, therefore, equal in resources with the best of the fund houses. There are only a limited number of ways by which price can be analyzed to make trade entries and exits. There is no system of technical analysis which can be said to be hundred per cent accurate and any conclusions drawn on the basis of technical analysis are, at best, an estimation of future probabilities. Despite these shortcomings, technical analysis, is still an objective and specific method of trading. **By using technical analysis, the trader is never in any doubt as to what his next course of action should be.** It's, however, another matter that only a few traders can put this knowledge to proper use for making money in the markets. Technical analysis is all about making calculated estimations regarding the future; and estimates can always go wrong. What is important for traders to recognize is that even at 50% estimation accuracy level, there can be handsome profits if their winning trades are larger than their losing ones.

A technical analyst first determines the trend of the market, or a stock, by using various tools, such as moving averages or trend lines, and then tries to trade in the direction of the trend by using indicators such as RSI which signal oversold or overbought conditions of the market.

It is almost impossible for traders to trade successfully without an understanding of technical analysis. Trading on the basis of fundamental analysis is an invitation to disaster.

~

3

~

The Fear of Getting Ruined

The possibility of getting ruined is real when you trade in the stock, commodities or any other financial markets. If you have started your trading career without first appropriately educating yourself, then you are, in fact, begging for it.

It is unfortunate that courses on financial literacy do not form any part of the educational curriculum in Indian schools and colleges at large except where specialized training is provided for financial advisors. Management of wealth, one of the most important aspects of everyone's life, is left aside whereas other important areas such as health and mathematics are taught vigorously. In the initial years of a career, very few people are really aware of terms like inflation and real interest rates. When the significance of these is understood later in life, it is often too late for starting a long term wealth management program which has the potential of providing high returns. When heroes are applauded in books, no emphasis is placed on the risk and training they undertook in attaining the glory. For example, Hillary and Tenzing are glorified as the first humans to scale Mount Everest whereas those who died trying the same feat are not even mentioned. When they climbed Everest, Tenzing and Hillary risked being killed by the extremely trying circumstances. To mitigate the risk, they trained themselves. Something which looks risky to the novice becomes a lower risk routine for the trained person.

The training (or learning) about something which seems risky removes the risk from it.

Furthermore, a lot of business news channels have a continuously running tape of stock prices and the changes in these prices from the previous day. Getting linked to a broker is also very easy. Trading can easily be done through the Internet and mobile phone. Tips are freely available on television and websites. Overall, the atmosphere for speculation is thus extremely compelling and omnipresent. In such a seemingly easy and inviting environment, only a few people would stop to think and accept that they need to educate themselves first.

The truth is that a lack of knowledge, combined with easy access to speculative markets, are the two most important causes of people getting ruined in trading.

Obviously, access to speculative markets cannot be restricted since these markets not only provide opportunities for trading but also provide hedging services to those who understand risk management strategies. The lack of knowledge is an issue which a person has to address himself.

If you plan to trade and are afraid of the risk of getting ruined, then I suggest the following:

1. Learn trading methods but do not start trading until you have found a method which is proven, profitable and personalized.

2. Estimate your capital requirement for trading depending upon your present earning capabilities and requirements and do not start trading until you have accumulated sufficient trading capital.

3. Since discipline forms an important component of trading success, you must "paper trade" your methods for a while, or

trade with only a small amount of money. Only once you find that you have been able to adhere to your methods, should you put your full capital in use. This sounds easy but in practice it has been observed that most traders take two to three years to overcome this hurdle. Since patience is an integral part of discipline and an important ingredient for trading success, it is suggested that you do not try to speed up the process lest it lead to avoidable losses and ruin.

4. Don't expect to make a killing. If you do, you may well be financially killed, instead.

Once you have gone through this book and understood risk management strategies, you will be a much wiser man. Then spend some time with other traders and discuss with them about their trading or investing methods. If you know someone who has been ruined by the stock markets, do not forget to include him or her in your survey. If possible, talk to your broker and ask him why most people lose money in the markets. You must focus on the following questions:

1. Do they use any specific methods of entries and exits? Some traders may not like to reveal their methods but it should be sufficient for you to know whether they have a well defined method or not.

2. Do they always exit their positions at pre-determined stop loss levels?

3. Do they keep changing their position size according to risk taking capacity or do they have some other method of calculating position size?

The answers to these questions should help you understand the causes of failure and this knowledge will be your most important tool for making a success of your foray into the stock market.

~

4

~

The Ingredients of Trading Success

I strongly believe that most successful traders should have a simple mechanical system of trading and that subjectivity must be avoided at all costs. Besides, every trader has his or her own personality traits, which have a direct bearing on his trading success. Many new traders feel that an intelligent grasp of technical methodology is sufficient in itself, but this is far from true. This becomes obvious to novices only after paying a heavy tuition in terms of money and time. If they have already lost their zeal and money during this period, then they may never appreciate this simple fact. Only a trader who has achieved success by adopting all of the reasonable inputs can realize the importance of personality in the trading game, ignoring which can be dangerous for the uninitiated.

Unfortunately it is also a widely held belief, more so in stock and commodity trading than in any other field, that luck and intuition have big roles in achieving success. While it is true that some people do seem to become astonishingly rich without appearing to have done much hard work, such cases are rare, maybe even illusory. However, these rare cases receive the widest publicity. The fact is that it is impossible to rely on luck and intuition in times of a crisis since both of these qualities are completely unpredictable. It is, therefore, imperative that traders devise reliable solutions which can be implemented in times of crises.

While a simple mechanical system is a basic requirement for solid and lasting trading success, it should not be taken to mean that creating such a system is also a simple task. Since the human mind is conditioned to attach more importance to things more complex, the first hurdle is that we get attracted to complex combinations of technical charts and indicators. The truth, however, is that unless we are able to discard needless complexity, we cannot hope to arrive at a simple strategy with any degree of confidence. On the other hand, systems such as simple crossovers of moving averages which keep you in the market at all times also need to be avoided because of the huge drawdowns which they entail when markets are not trending. What is really needed is a system which is not only based on solid criteria and established principles of technical analysis, but is also not unnecessarily complex. Thus:

- If a system does not follow the established principles, it is a statistical failure from the start.
- If a system meets the established principles but is overly complex, then while it may be statistically successful the personality of the trader will not let it succeed.

Therefore, those new to technical analysis and trading should not expect that the expositions in this book are going to be easy to assimilate although professional traders and determined novice traders will ultimately be greatly rewarded for their persistence. I suggest that all traders must consider themselves as perennial students to achieve success in stock market, particularly if they are going to use technical analysis. The methods in this book are not difficult to understand for those having a basic knowledge of technical analysis.

Ultimately, a system must be proven by historical data as well as real time performance. One major difference between history and real time is that history is not impacted by the trader's personality or the emotions that come into play when real money is on the line. The drawdown periods in historical data are often ignored in favor of the overall net profits which the system shows. But, in real time, the ability to bear an extended period of drawdown is what makes or mars a trader. Not having adequate capital may be one of the reasons that panics a trader during drawdowns, but it is the loss of confidence in one's trading system which eventually seals the fate of even highly capitalized traders. What can be done to improve this confidence? Perhaps, not much. One reason for my pessimistic view is that most traders are in a hurry to make big profits — and when expected profits do not materialize due to inexperience and lack of patience, the trader drifts off to other ideas, forsaking his own well researched and proven system. That is why it has been said that two to three years are required to become a confident trader and it is suggested that novice traders do not try to speed up the process.

Eventually, the ambitions of a trader will determine his or her level of determination and nobody should be led to believe that this seemingly simple business is indeed simple. The amount of money that can be made in futures trading is fantastically large and this arena has always attracted some of the most intelligent and enterprising people from all walks of life. Therefore, a novice should rightly expect fierce competition rather than an empty playground. It is said: "If you can hold your head above the water when all the others are drowning, then indeed you are a man!" That's very true in trading. Is there then any hope for you if you are the type who has always been risk averse? Yes, there is, if you understand that risk comes from the unknown and knowledge makes the unknown familiar and helps in eliminating the fear of risk from your mind. More fearful a person, the more training or learning he requires to eliminate that fear.

Much hindrance has been caused to the learning process due to the noise about markets being rational or efficient. One class of traders may feel more inclined towards the efficient market theory and is therefore happy to achieve market related returns. Another class of traders, although not in awe of the efficient market theory, feels that there is nothing much that can be learnt beyond fundamental analysis. Their attempts to beat the market are thus generally thwarted due to a lack of faith in past history and a constant feeling that the times are now "different." An element of luck is also required to succeed for those depending upon intuition, or even fundamental analysis, since it is impossible to know at any time all the fundamentals affecting the future. Fundamental analysis is, therefore, best left for those who have huge resources at their command and are often privy to inside news.

Another class of traders is the one who have acquired some knowledge of technical analysis but are confused by the number of techniques, indicators, etc. available. Should one be a contrarian and sell on negative divergences? Or, must one follow the trend till the market throws one out? Which of the oscillators is the right one? Should one choose an RSI of 7 periods or 14 periods? Will the system work in a changed market scenario?

Lastly, there are traders who have been successfully using technical analysis in their trading but have realized that discipline and money management rules are far more important than better entry and exit points. O'Shaughnessy in his famous book, *What Works on Wall Street* has proved it beyond doubt that even the most intelligent mutual fund managers are prone to failure due to their inability to follow their own systems in a disciplined manner. And discipline in trading is not easy to come by.

> Whatever may have been said or written about the efficient market theory, one thing is clear to any experienced trader: the markets are extremely efficient in transferring wealth from the indisciplined to the disciplined!

One ought to remember at all times that a system derives its power from the statistically proven historical track record, and for statistics to work in real time, patience and strict adherence to rules are required. If you know that a system may give ten losing trades in a row then you will not be unnerved by your sixth or seventh loss, nor give up on the system.

What if the trader is not aware of the potential loss his next trade might cause? If a trader buys a fixed quantity of stock at every signal and his stop loss rules are ad-hoc — e.g., sometimes the stop loss is close by and at other times it is far away — then he will lose a disproportionate amount in some of his trades. If, for example, the previous five trades have been losers then an element of fear may crop up if the sixth trade presents itself with a rather large stop loss. The trade may then be avoided — and then it turns out to have been a profitable move! Every trader frequently faces these situations and it is best to start your trading program only after finding answers to these questions. Whether a trading position should be based on equal share, equal rupee, or equal risk — the three different methods of position sizing — is not a matter of arbitrary choice but is dependent upon the system you've chosen for making your trade entries and exits. For example, if a trader is using moving average crossovers for entries and exits, then the equal risk method of position sizing will not work in his favor.

If the criteria for money management and position sizing are clearly laid out and followed then one of the biggest perils of trading, namely overtrading, also gets automatically eliminated.

Have Realistic Expectations

Most investors in India who enter the market during bull phases have unrealistic expectations of achieving extraordinary returns even with a simple buy and hold strategy and using the simplest of portfolios, i.e. an index fund.

Investors should not forget that interest rates on bank deposits in India are now governed more by market forces rather than being decided by the central government. Earlier, for a long time, high interest rates on bank deposits were the norm. Because the stock market generally tends to provide returns higher than the prevailing interest rates, a return of 18%, namely a return 5% to 6% above the then prevalent interest rates was possible. One should remember that developed markets, such as USA, where the bank interest rates are generally below 3%, have failed to provide even 10% per annual returns in the last two to three decades. This is due to the subtle phenomenon of risk premium which tends to limit the overall returns. In general, more risky an asset is, higher should be the potential return from owning it. The least risky asset is a government bond since it comes with a sovereign guarantee and hence the yield on these bonds is the minimum available. Bank deposits are slightly more risky and hence they provide slightly higher returns as compared to government bonds. Corporate bonds are even more risky and also provide much higher returns than do bank deposits. Stocks and shares of companies are most risky investments and thus are expected to provide much higher returns. Higher the available interest rates on risk free investments, higher would be the risk premium expected by investors holding riskier assets. Therefore, in India, when interest rates on bank deposits were more than 10% per annum, it was reasonable to expect returns of 18% or more per annum from stock markets but with interest rates hovering around 6% to 7% in recent years, a more reasonable figure would be 12% to 15%. These expectations are for holding an investment for the long term. So far as a trader is concerned, the returns would depend more on his skill than on the prevailing interest rates.

It was not just the bank interest rate differential between developed countries and India, which still persists to some extent although the difference is getting narrower, that was responsible for higher returns in the past; there were other factors as well. Due to the load of paper work involved, along with the resultant bad deliveries and floor based trading where only exchange members were allowed to trade on behalf of the clients, few Indian investors were willing to exit stocks they held. They were simply not sure of getting the right price from their brokers. There is no doubt that many brokers would extract the maximum from their clients. In fact, they would charge way beyond a justifiable brokerage fee by taking advantage of the closed-door nature of the exchanges. With the advent of dematerialization, low brokerage fees and transparent screen based trading platforms, there are now fewer truly long term investors. This tendency has resulted in rapid turnover of shares and there is almost always adequate supply of stock at most quoted prices. In short, market efficiency has improved so much that the Indian market can now be considered to be at par with the best stock markets of the world.

The introduction of futures and options in Nifty indices has also enabled intelligent investors to hedge their portfolios, once again bringing Indian markets at par with the more developed ones.

However, before the introduction of all these changes in 2003, the Indian markets were not considered tradable by FIIs and large institutional investors. Large inflow of dollars has since hiked the valuations of Indian markets even higher than the developed markets. This, in part, was due to India's high GDP growth but re-rating of Indian stocks was also a factor.

The purpose of highlighting these changes is to alert the reader not to expect the past levels of returns in the future as well, since the highly advanced, efficient, already re-rated Indian market is now a part of the global market scenario. Thus, for example, events in USA, the largest economy of the world, have a large bearing on India.

Readers will be well served by keeping their expectations realistic and by focusing attention on controlling risk instead. Reasonable expectations coupled with proper risk management skills will keep one stress free. Then, whenever the markets decide to reward you with spectacular returns, you would be in a position to take advantage of such opportunities. This, perhaps, is the key to success. **The whole purpose of doing a business, even stock trading, is to maximize profits but if the stress level is high, the trader is likely to get burnt out which will then result in poor trading decisions.** It is not possible to take level headed decisions in a highly stressful environment. The ultimate returns are as much dependent upon your own well being as they are dependent upon sound trading methodology.

~

5

~

Trader *versus* Investor

It is not just a failed trader who becomes an investor. The circumstances of a person play a decisive role in making a choice between trading and investing. Time constraints may not allow a person to trade effectively since trading requires stringent controls on capital management on a day-to-day or, sometimes, hour-to-hour basis. One of the major psychological advantages of being an investor is that the requirement of discipline is not that severe. If an investment goes down in value, it is often not considered by the investor as a failure of his investing method but simply an opportunity to buy more if capital is available. If an investor decides to follow rupee cost averaging (RCA), then the burden of discipline is taken away altogether. Otherwise, a lot of subjectivity is required in the process of selecting an investment and frequently the short term behavior of a stock may even be in the opposite direction to the perceived value. Due to the large number of fundamental influences which affect stock prices in an unpredictable manner, some intuition or hunch is almost always an integral part of an investment process.

For example, the Reserve Bank of India declares its monetary policy every quarter which sets the tone for the interest rates. An increase of the rate by 0.25% may be considered bearish by some investors as it increases the cost of capital for companies, while other investors may choose to ignore the news altogether on the ground that higher growth rates would take care of the increase in interest rates. It is very difficult to decide which of the above groups will eventually be proved correct. But the one who is ultimately proved right is the one who was right in the beginning too! However, the same logic (or was it a hunch?) may not work the next time when similar conditions prevail once again.

A trader, on the other hand, can't afford to be indisciplined or even dare to use a hunch. If a trader has a proven system and then superimposes his hunches on that then he is circumventing his own system and he will not get the desired returns. If a trader has no proven system and trades entirely on the basis of hunch, then he is inviting failure right from the start. There may be an odd trader or two who has amassed wealth on a continuous basis by using his hunches but such a trader is a rare bird.

Therefore the most important distinction between a trader and an investor is their varying needs to be disciplined. For a trader, discipline is the difference between survival and ruin.

Why is this so? Firstly, most successful traders trade on both the long as well as the short side of the market. If a trader does not exit a short position on a pre-determined stop loss level then he may face a big drawdown, impairing his capacity to trade effectively. Secondly, most traders use leverage, i.e. margin trading facility, to generate meaningful returns and often do not have the capital to consider their long positions, now falling in value, as long term investments. Strict adherence to position size, trade management and stop losses is a must if a trader wants to remain solvent. On the other hand, investors do not short sell and use very little, if any, leverage. The possibility of ruin is thus avoided. In the worst case scenario, the maximum an investor may lose is his invested capital, unlike in the case of a trader who may be required to meet margin calls even beyond his available capital.

In short, without discipline, a trader risks becoming an investor and that too, a bad one!

Of course, it is not necessary to compartmentalize people into categories such as investors or traders. An investor can be a trader too, and *vice versa*. It must, however, be clearly understood that investing and trading are two entirely distinct activities, requiring separate sets of strategies and skills, and the two should not be mixed up. If a trader wants also to have an investment portfolio, then he should maintain separate accounts and should judge the performance of each activity separately. This is necessary since wrong conclusions may be drawn and a good trading strategy may be abandoned due to poor performance of the investment portfolio — or, *vice versa*.

~

6

~

News, Views and Tips

One of the paradoxes of investing or trading success is that more the amount of information assimilated by an investor, less are his chances of making a success in the stock market.

The reason perhaps lies in the fact that the "eyes do not see what the mind does not know." For example, a reduction in a company's inventory level of a company may signal a turnaround but such news may not be analyzed properly if the investor is not aware of its significance. The investor or trader may place undue importance to dollar inflows of FIIs (Foreign Financial Institutions) while choosing to ignore company specific news and then is dismayed if the price doesn't move in the desired direction. Efficient market theorists will tell you that all news gets immediately discounted, i.e. reflected in the price, leaving little possibility of deriving any benefit from buying or selling a share on the basis of such news. However, if you are trading on the basis of technical analysis, you are most likely going to have a position on the right side of the market when such news comes.

For example, consider the breakout on 18 May 2009 when the market had even to be closed for one hour as soon as it opened with an upside gap of 10%. While it may have been a surprise move due to Congress party unexpectedly returning to power without the support of Communist parties, those following sound technical trading methods would already have been a part of this move.

Figure 6.1 depicts an hourly chart of Nifty futures showing that the 8-hour MA (moving average) line had gone below the 21-hour MA line on 11 May 2009. The 13-day MA line was also above the 34-day MA line at this point (not shown) so the daily trend was up. Traders using the system described in this book would have been trying to establish a long position on the breakout of a swing high. Such a swing had been created at the Nifty level of 3,717 on 8 May 2009 and this was broken on the upside on 13 May 2009. The trader would have gone long at this level

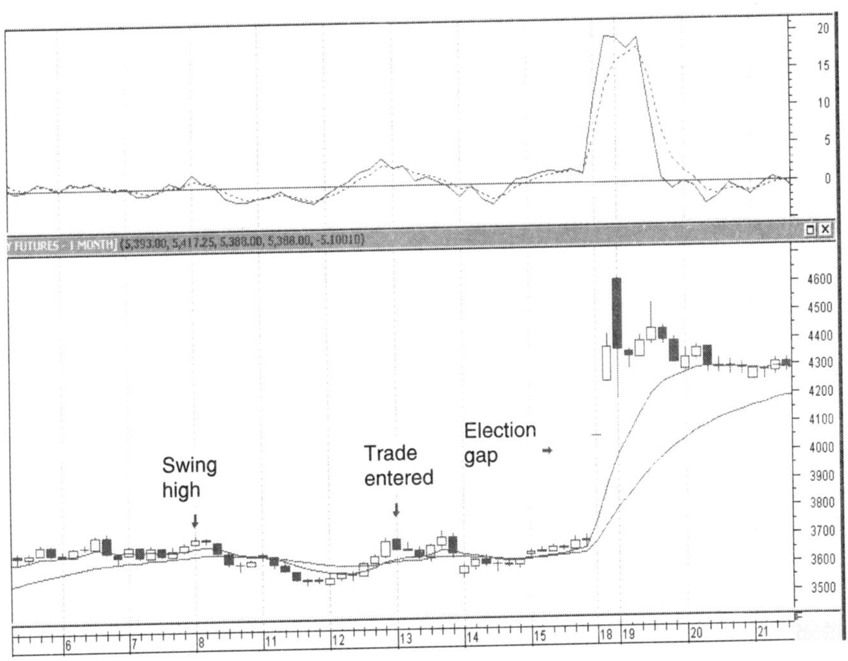

Figure 6.1: **Hourly chart of Nifty futures for 18 May 2009**

with a stop loss of 3,532 created on 11 May 2009. As per our trading system, he would have been in the trade when the market made the huge gap and would have ridden the trade till at the level of 4,163, thus generating extraordinary profits.

There is no doubt that as many traders were short in futures as were long when the market made this big jump and those who were short would have lost quite a bit of money during the same period. Some may not have had a sound method to begin with. Besides, any method can sometimes give an extraordinarily large loss.

Nevertheless, talk about people losing their capital in the market due to some news event is quite frequent. The fact is that traders and investors get ruined only when they overtrade and when they do not pay heed to their stop losses.

GDP and Stock Prices

Some traders seem to attach a lot of significance to minor variations of GDP (Gross Domestic Product) numbers but here again no extra benefit can be availed so far as trading is concerned. The important question for the trader is the price he should pay for the stock he wants to own. The price is here and now, and not in some distant future. It is very unlikely that a trader would be the first one to know about rising or falling GDP. Stock prices would probably already have discounted, i.e. accounted for, this factor. Perhaps the prices have already reached a peak and GDP growth may become stagnant or may even start falling in the future. Perhaps the future growth in GDP may be more due to unlisted companies or due to agriculture. It is also possible that the company in whose share the trader is interested may issue more stock to meet its expansion needs, thus diluting any benefit that may occur to previous or new traders.

It is useful to keep in mind the old adage, "Sell on good news, buy on bad news." Actually, in general, the best action would be to not act on news. If you feel compelled to do something, then it's better for an investor to be a contrarian and buy stocks when the GDP is falling and when they are available near their liquidation value, or even below that!

For example, the Japanese stock market index reached a peak of 40,000 in 1990. Japan's GDP was then rising at a very handsome rate and it was anticipated that Japan would even overtake USA as a financial power. Investors suspended all judgment of sane stock valuations and bought heavily. Once prices started falling, these investors didn't get to see the equivalent of their purchase prices even after a passage of twenty years! The same happened with the Chinese stock market as shown in Figure 6.2.

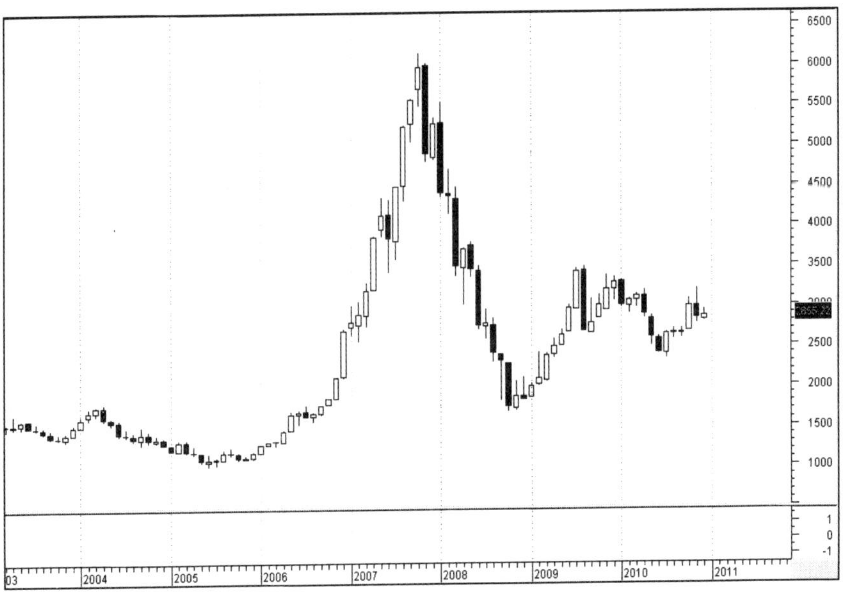

Figure 6.2: **Chart showing how the Shanghai index (index of Chinese stock market) was available at less than half of its price in 2010 as compared to its price in 2007, even though Chinese GDP growth was still more than 9% at the end of 2010.**

~

Mergers and Acquisitions (M&A)

There are strategies which are designed to take advantage of mergers and acquisitions but the problem is that typically M&A news reaches investors quite late and so the benefits, if any, are small. Furthermore, such events are quite infrequent in India and any investment or trading based on such news should be considered as purely speculative. In any case, there is no need to be overly optimistic about the results of mergers or acquisitions since the overall outcome of such a scenario is more likely to be bad than good for the companies concerned. The reason for this is that most such activities tend to take place when the valuations are already quite stretched and the acquiring company's stock is more likely to fall rather than rise after the acquisition. So far as the company being acquired is concerned, insider trading will ensure that the price of its stock would already have risen to discount for the acquisition even before the news become public.

If a trader has a proven strategy without the need of factoring in news related to such events, then he is better off sticking with his strategy rather than just waiting for some news to trigger his trade.

Interest Rates

A low interest rate regime is conducive to the healthy growth of companies because of reduced recurring expenditure and low interest cost of expansion plans. However, low interest rates generally prevail in a gloomy economic atmosphere when the demand for money is low. Low interest rates are also a key feature of economic recessions. At such times, stock prices keep making new lows with each passing day and very few investors are really keen on buying stocks. Actually, however, this is the best time to buy stocks of good companies for investment. The old adage, "Buy when there is blood on the street," applies to this kind of a situation.

Nevertheless, any buying at such junctures is quite risky in the short term and hence not at all advisable for traders. You may buy at such junctures with a long term investment point of view and must not use any leverage for such long positions.

Company Results and Announcements

Most traders would have noticed that whenever a company announces its financial results, business news channels on TV also mention the difference between the profits which the analysts estimated and the actual profits made by the company. I have noticed that these analyst estimates are usually quite accurate.

Why is this so? The reason is that mutual fund houses, foreign financial institutions (FIIs) and large brokerage houses have at their disposal experienced and knowledgeable analysts whose main business is to track a particular sector of the economy. They are trained to look at and absorb news which an ordinary investor would hardly be able to interpret. Besides, these analysts also visit companies to evaluate what is happening there. Thus, other than company insiders, these analysts are usually the first ones to know things which may have significance for the stock price of that company. Their reports are then made available to their bosses who are the big buyers on the street. Only after these bosses — usually the managers of mutual funds and foreign financial institutions — are done with their buying or selling, is the analyst's report released to the public. Remember that these analysts are not paid by you and, so, if their reports are first made available to you, why should their current bosses pay them any salary?

In a nutshell, little trading purpose will be served by looking for financial results or announcements related to stock splits, bonus shares, dividends, launching of a new product, withdrawal of a previous product, change of managing director, etc., because either the benefits occurring from these are insignificant, or no benefits can be drawn due to the news having already been discounted.

Money in stock markets is not made by the more intelligent — but by those who have the courage and confidence to adhere to their simple, but proven, strategies.

Views and Tips

"Making money on free advice is like winning a lottery without buying a ticket." How likely is that?

What about analysts who are airing their views on TV channels and providing free tips as well? Are they not speaking the truth? Do they have any ulterior motive in giving free tips? Do they have some superior forecasting ability?

When an analyst makes a statement regarding the future movement of a stock, he is giving the audience a well considered opinion. He may also mention the price at which entry should be made, along with the probable price target and stop loss. But before acting on such tips, ask yourself whether you have confidence in the analyst making the statement. Have you carefully understood the risk and reward ratio of his tip? Have you considered the time frame required to hold the trade on the basis of the given tip? Will it have any adverse, or beneficial, effect on your existing portfolio? Do you have the capital required to carry the trade till the exit suggested by the analyst? Has the price already moved beyond the entry price being suggested, thus skewing the risk and reward ratio unfavorably? Can you depend upon the analyst for regular tips, or for making suitable adjustments in the trade as it progresses?

It is better to paper trade — for at least 100 trades or 3 months — on the basis of tips and only then should you draw any conclusions about the viability of this option.

~

7
~
Beware the Myth that "This Time It's Different!"

"This time it is different,!" is a remark that is often heard at bullish and bearish extremes of the market. History has proved time and again that this fallacy is one of the most common causes of ruin. Not only that. There are hardly any instances when some benefits could have been derived from this phrase, especially in the stock market. If anything, it only indicates the need for taking a contrarian view.

All financial markets where speculation is allowed are driven partly by the fundamentals and partly by sentiment. It is a fact that when fundamentals have played out their role, the sentiment may still point in the same direction. Consider, for example, that a raging bull market is in progress due to rising corporate profits coupled with low interest rates. During such periods, any reduction in corporate profits, or a rise in interest rates, may be completely ignored by market participants, at least in the beginning. In fact, it is a characteristic of the last stage of a bull market that most bad news, even important one, is ignored whereas even minor good news leads to a further rise in price. The human mind is such that information which confirms one's own opinion is given significance whereas the opposite viewpoint may be vehemently rejected. Furthermore, to justify the ever growing optimism — or pessimism, as the case may be — new theories are put forward by market leaders.

During the dot-com mania in 1999-2000, website companies were getting valued not by the dollars they earned but by the number of eyeballs the website attracted. Most of these dot-com companies eventually disappeared, along with their share value. Why did eyeballs, instead of dollars, become such a useful tool for valuing shares of such companies? It was because the investor sentiment was at that time being driven by the ever rising share prices of these stocks and investors were eager to latch on to any explanation for the absurd prices. Eventually, the bubble burst. In India, many companies such as DSQ Software, Silverline Industries, etc. almost disappeared from the stock markets. The share price of Pentamedia, for example, fell to less than ₹3 (no, this is not a printing error!) from a high of ₹2,344 (*see* Figure 7.1).

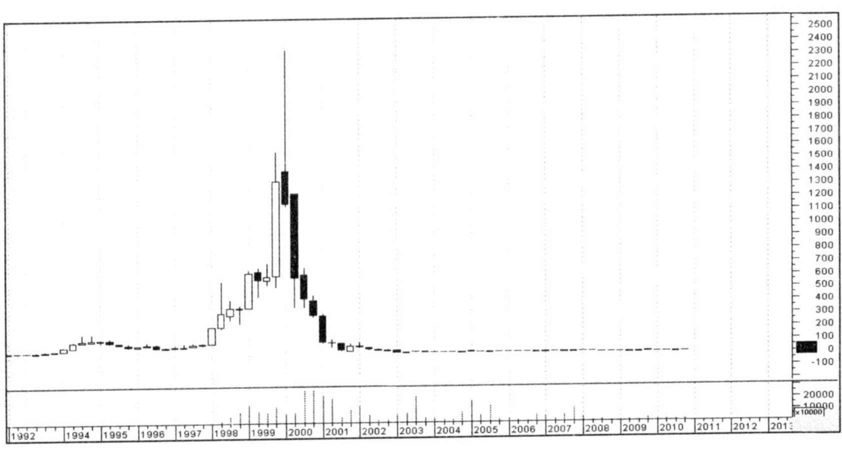

Figure 7.1: **Quarterly chart of Pentamedia Graphics showing its steep rise — and an equally steep fall — during the dot-com boom and bust.**

~

But there are also those who are driven by level-headed calculation rather than herd mentality. When most investors were deliriously making three digit returns during the dot-com boom, Warren Buffett was criticized for not having any software stocks in his portfolio and thus depriving his shareholders of big gains. He held on to his formula of buying high quality stocks at less than fair price — what he calls as his "margin of safety" — and turned out to be a big winner when the dot-com bubble later burst. When asked why he did not have any software stocks in his portfolio, he remarked, "Because I don't understand them!"

In India at that time, a stock operator by the name of Ketan Parekh was considered to be the most important proponent of the phrase, "This time it's different." He also backed his opinion by heavily buying software stocks. Those who believed him rued their fate for years. The difference is that he bought with money that was not his own, while other investors had to buy the same stocks with their own hard earned money. Before that, Harshad Mehta was considered to be the architect of the bull run of the 1992. He, too, used others' money to play his nefarious game. Ketan Parekh used to be one of his associates. The only difference between the two was that while Harshad Mehta misused money from public sector banks, Ketan Parekh did the same with money from co-operative banks. Both misused money which was entrusted to them by banks for other purposes. Both were big risk takers and, in the process, ruined themselves. But to say that the investing public got ruined due to these people is giving too much credit to this infamous duo. People got ruined due to the same reasons as these two were ruined — over trading.

Human memory is, however, short and new events unfolding at a fast pace smother the memory of earlier ones. The stock market had made its peak in February 2000 and started to fall thereafter. It made a bottom in September 2001. Although most outside observers attributed this fall to the attack on World Trade

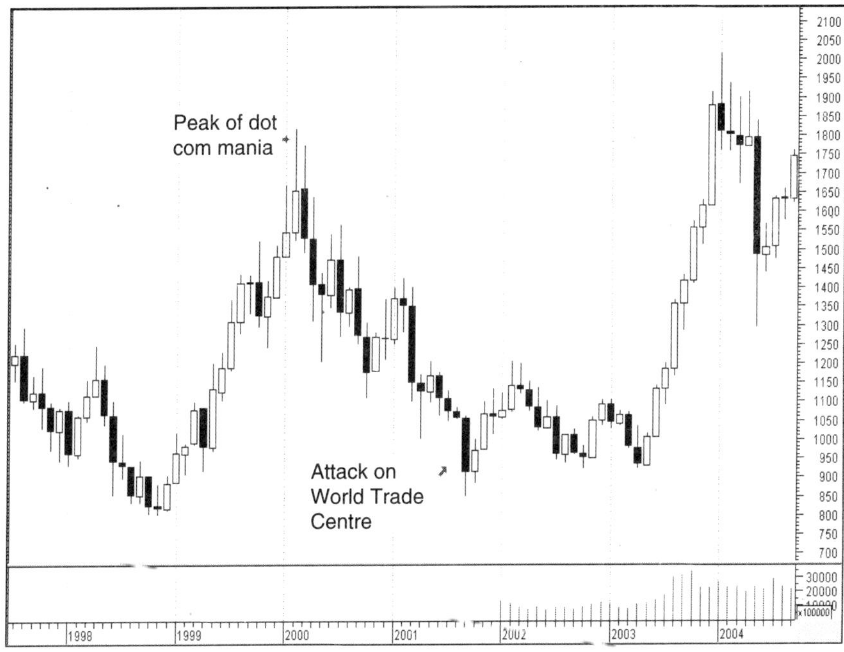

Figure 7.2: **Nifty made a peak of 1,818 in February 2000 and then started falling. It fell to a low of 850 in the month of September 2001 when World Trade Center in New York was attacked.**

~

Center (WTC), it was not really so. Only the terminal 20% fall can be attributed to that terror attack because markets all over the world had started falling steeply after the February 2000 peak and the bear market had already been in progress for more than one-and-half years when WTC was attacked. Most investors liquidated their long held portfolios of stocks in panic fearing that the end of the world was near.

In fact, the market was then offering a never before buying opportunity to those who kept their nerves. The phrase, "this time it is different," was interpreted in a contrasting manner by two classes of investors. One class sold its stocks at whatever

Figure 7.3: **Monthly chart of Nifty from 2002 to 2010**

~

price they could, while another group bought the stocks then available at throwaway prices. This latter group was of the opinion that such an opportunity comes only once in lifetime and that is why "this time it was different."

Did it then take a long time for the investors to realize that times are never different in stock markets? The answer is no, as the chart in Figure 7.3 reveals.

After having made a bottom in September 2001, the Nifty remained in accumulation mode till mid-2003. A long term bull market took off from there which ultimately peaked in February 2008.

During this period, India — along with China, most notably, and some other emerging markets — saw a continuously high growth in its Gross Domestic Product (GDP). The market was also supported by high domestic consumption and huge inflows of foreign funds through FIIs. Some investors and traders attach a lot of significance to recent FII purchases as if that is enough proof of intelligence. They forget that FIIs are happy to generate 6% to 10% per annum since interest rates in their own country are not more than 3%. Indian investors must remember that they, on the other hand, can easily earn 7% from bank deposits without any risk. Besides, FIIs can also take advantage of any favorable currency exchange rates. The thing to understand is that a prudent buyer of stocks would like to accumulate them during a quiet period in the market and if FII purchases in the market are big enough for the market to make new highs, then it stands to reason that most of the gains have already been made.

Real estate companies were then in limelight as well as some other sectors but shares of companies like Hindustan Unilever, ITC, etc. were not very fashionable during this period. Most investors were told that India had been lagging behind the developed countries for a long time and was now only catching up with them. Since it would take a long time for India to actually catch up, therefore there was no reason why the country's GDP growth should slow in the future. Thus, the narrative went that the absurd market P/E levels and the low dividend yield should not be a matter of concern because "this time it is different!"

Around this time, Indians also got the new experience of shopping in malls which were a phenomenon of this phase of the market. Many of the malls turned out to be complete financial disasters but the stocks of the companies owning these malls were highly recommended by analysts. Their main reasoning was that it did not matter how much money was being made — or lost, actually! — by these malls; what mattered was the "footfalls" they attracted. Remember eyeballs of the dot-com era? Ah! How soon those "eyeballs" were forgotten!

"The companies fuelling this rally are not some garage based dot-com companies of old but solid brick and mortar companies and the prices of the stocks are justified by the assets (land and buildings) the companies own," investors were told. Not only that. Due to the increasing transparency in Indian stock markets, combined with government's liberal policies, the confidence of foreign institutional investors was said to be growing and a re-rating of the Indian stock market was supposedly taking place. Investors were requested to ignore the previous criteria of stock valuation lest they miss the upcoming big profits.

Not a single investor could have imagined at that time that the stock of the largest real estate company in India, DLF, would be

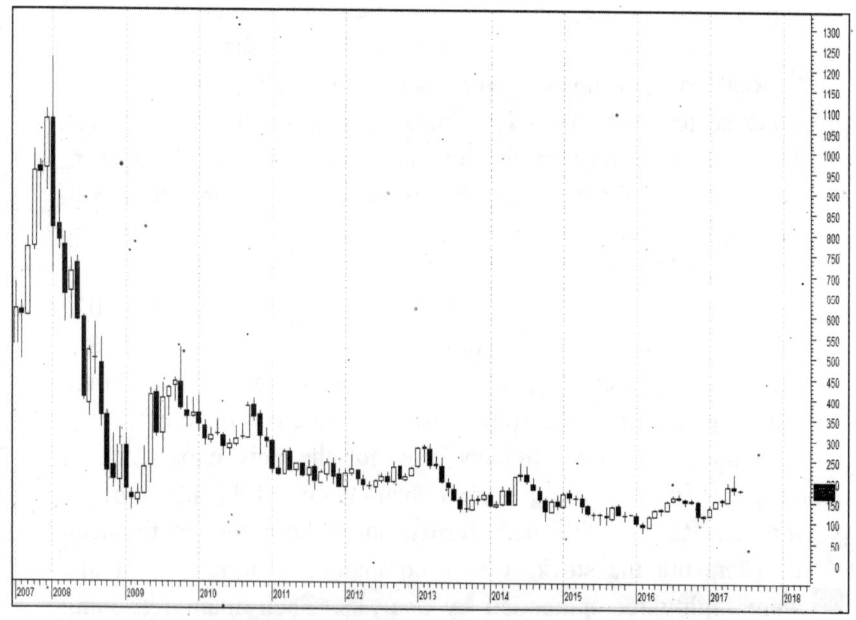

Figure 7.4: **Monthly chart of DLF, a leader in India's real estate segment. DLF reached a high of ₹1,225 in February 2008 — and was available for ₹175 in 2017.**

~

available a year later at one-tenth of its price. Yes, DLF fell 90% from its peak of February 2008 — within a year! It would be a long time, if ever, that an early investor in DLF would break even (*see* Figure 7.4).

What was different at the time of the February 2008 high? Nothing, but the same old herd mentality and greed in a different garb!

When there was Internet mania,
All that we cared for was eyeball;
During the real estate bubble,
We were told to look for footfall;
When there was neither mania nor bubble,
What we had was free fall!

When Nifty made a bottom of 2,253 in October 2008, very few investors were looking at the cheap valuations at which blue chip companies were then available. All eyes were focused on American investment banks and all minds were busy speculating which bank would fail next. The times were really different this time, said the doomsayers! The whole banking system would collapse and all foreign money would flow out of India! India's GDP growth would stagnate and God knows what else would happen! In fact, the period from October 2008 to March 2009 turned out to be the best time ever for building a portfolio of solid blue chip companies at throwaway prices (*see* Figure 7.5).

I can fill many more pages by giving historic examples of the Tulip mania of Holland, South Sea bubble, the gold mania, etc., but I have confined myself only to the recent history of the Indian stock market because I have witnessed it first hand. Besides, the follies of our recent era are sufficient to prove that while the apparent causes may look different, it is the herd contagion of greed and fear which ultimately drives markets to their extremes. Investors who take a cool, calculated approach, which is often

Figure 7.5: **Monthly chart of Nifty showing the bull market that began in October 2008**

~

contrarian, are handsomely rewarded for their effort and discipline. So far as the other investors are concerned, the less we concern ourselves with them, the better we are.

The point is simple. Whenever you think, or are told that — "This time it's different!" — immediately remind yourself of the other equally popular phrase, "Sell on good news, buy on bad news," and then evaluate the prevalent market conditions. If you harbour a trader's mentality, you will be in a better position to take advantage of such opportunities.

~

Part 2

~

The Essentials of Trading

8

Averaging is Not a Trading Technique

If the price of a stock which has been bought starts falling, there are only three alternatives. An active trader may like to exit the trade at a pre-determined stop loss. A passive investor may choose to do nothing, while an active investor may consider it to be an opportunity for averaging down.

It must be noted that averaging techniques can only be profitable when an investment is intended for the long term.

The use of leverage must be avoided while implementing any of these strategies because the interest and brokerage cost of frequent rollovers may take away much of the profits from averaging strategies. Remember, also, that the aim of these strategies is to generate a higher return than that available from a simple buy and hold strategy and to reduce the risk of investing by spreading the investment over a period of time.

Stop loss, on the other hand, is an indispensable survival technique for traders. Traders are not looking to beat inflation over the long term but are in the markets to "make a killing," here and now. It's another matter that 95% of the traders are not even able to survive in the markets for more than a year.

To make a killing, traders have to go long in bull markets and go short in bear markets.

If they are long and the price starts going down, they have two choices. Either they can exit and protect their remaining capital, or they can buy even more stock to average out their buying price. The former strategy would require a stop loss technique while the latter strategy would require an averaging technique, plus the availability of extra capital. But traders do not have an infinite amount of capital and usually they do not have the patience to wait long term because their brokers are always breathing down their necks for depositing mark-to-market losses. The same can also happen in the case of a short position with an even worse outcome since it may still be possible to think of a long position as a long term investment in the hope that prices will come to "sanity" some day but a short position will have to be covered eventually as the prices do not have an upper limit, although they cannot go lower than zero. Theoretically, the risk on a short position is unlimited while the gains are limited. That is why it has been said:

One who sells what is not hissen,
Must either buy it back or go to prison.

Traders also need to work with high leverage to generate reasonable returns. After all, how much can a market move in a short span? For example, the average daily range of Nifty futures is usually less than 150. Hence, a trader can expect to make or lose a maximum of 150 points on the Nifty in one day but it is not possible for a trader to enter at the lowest level and exit at the highest level. The average range for a one-year period is approximately 1,500. So, in theory, it is possible to make or lose 15% if you were to hold Nifty for one year but it is not possible to make the same percentage if you were to hold Nifty for 7 days. Thus, traders work on margin in order to make money. They put in 10% to 20% of their trading position and the rest is borne by the broker (or the exchange). The high leverage assures bigger profits if their analysis is good and, conversely, bigger losses if their analysis is incorrect.

To protect themselves from ruin, traders use the stop loss techniques since, typically, they do not have the financial strength to average. But some traders do not use stop loss techniques and instead go on averaging in the hope that eventually the market will come to their rescue. Such traders form 95% part of the overall trading community who go out of trading every year and then blame the markets for their misfortune. On the other hand, **successful traders focus their attention on preservation of capital through the correct and prudent use of stop loss techniques** and it is on this topic that we shall focus our attention in the next chapter.

~

9
~
Stop Loss

Stop loss is the single most important tool in a trader's armory.

Nothing is more important for a trader than stop loss. A stop loss is the price level at which a trader would exit his position to prevent further erosion of his capital.

Estimated Stop Loss and Actual Stop Loss

A stop loss order is an instruction given to a broker specifying the level at which the trader would like to exit his position.

Suppose a trader is long one contract of Nifty futures with the Nifty level at 10,000. The trader reckons that if Nifty goes below 9,930 then his analysis of a rising trend in Nifty would have been proved wrong and it would then be better to exit the trade at a small loss rather than risk taking a bigger loss later on. Accordingly, he would ask the broker to place a stop loss at 9,930. **We call this the estimated stop loss.**

In practice, however, the stop loss should be placed a little lower than 9,930, say, for example, at 9,925. **We call this the actual stop loss.**

How much difference should there be between your estimated stop loss and the actual stop loss given to the broker? That depends on the liquidity (volume) of the share or security and the time frame being traded. In Nifty, this difference may be 0.05% if the trader is trading on intraday time frame with 15-minute to 60-minute charts and 0.2% if the traded time frame is daily.

For example, if the estimated stop loss in Nifty futures is 9,930, then the actual stop loss should be 9,925 for an intraday trade time frame and 9,910 if the trade is on a daily time frame. In stock futures, however, the difference should be at least 0.25% for intraday time frame trades and 1% for daily time frame trades because individual stocks are more volatile and also less liquid than index and hence their prices can show larger changes as compared to Nifty due to the relatively smaller transactions in the market. So far as illiquid future contacts are concerned, the simple advice is not to trade them.

Also:

- A sell stop loss is entered when you want to exit a long position, or if you want to create a short position; and
- A buy stop loss is entered when you want to exit a short position, or you want to create a long position.

How to Determine Stop Loss Levels

There are several methods of determining stop loss levels and the choice of method, depends on the strategy employed for making trade entries and also the capital which can be put at risk on any given trade.

For example, if a trader follows the moving average crossovers to make entries, then a crossover in the opposite direction will decide the exit. In such cases, there is no predetermined stop loss level since the price at which the opposite crossover will take place is not known in advance. The same also holds true if MACD signals are used to make entries. But the trading system discussed in this book does not allow any entry until a stop loss has become clearly defined. Therefore, the trader is never in any doubt regarding his estimated stop loss. He only needs to calculate the actual stop loss, the strike price and the trigger price to feed the order. Furthermore, all entries in this system are made only on breakouts and breakdowns and hence are done through the use of buy and sell stop losses.

One important advantage of using such a system is that the trader can calculate his position size exactly as per the capital he wants to put at risk, something which is not possible for systems that use moving average crossovers for entries and exits. This will be further elaborated upon later in the book.

In my opinion, stop losses should serve both purposes, namely they should help avoid bigger than estimated losses and they should also reflect market psychology. A bigger than acceptable loss will jeopardize a trader's survival in the market and a stop loss which has been determined without paying attention to support and resistance levels will force the trader to exit a trade prematurely and thus will preempt any chances of making expected profits. In the case of a long position, this would mean placing the stop loss below a well defined pivot point — and *vice versa* for a short position.

The level of stop loss on a long position should be such that it marks a point where most of the traders would turn bearish. Correspondingly, the stop loss on a short position should be such that the market is likely to turn bullish if the stop loss is hit. If the stop loss is not decided by keeping these factors in mind then it may get hit by minor market noise, thus throwing the trader out of a trade prematurely, i.e. when the trade still has a long way to go.

Initial Stop Loss and Trailing Stop Loss

A stop loss defined at the time of entering a trade is known as an initial stop loss. If the trade does not progress any further, this stop loss may be hit by an adverse price move which may throw the trader out of the market at a loss.

On the other hand, if the price moves favorably then it is entirely possible that another swing low / swing high may be created providing the trader with a more favorable stop loss than the initial one. Such **a subsequent favorable stop loss is called a trailing stop loss**. Eventually if the price moves significantly in a favorable manner, the trailing stop loss may get shifted to successively higher, or lower, levels as the case may be, where even if the stop loss is hit the trade would be exited in profit.

What about Targets?

Why discuss targets in a chapter on stop loss? Because booking profit based on pre-determined profit targets may prevent erosion of paper profits. In the stock market it pays to respect your paper profits in the same manner as you respect your real profits.

There is no doubt that profits can be enhanced by calculating targets for a trade but this requires considerable experience. Fibonacci ratios such as 1.618 and 2.618 are often used to calculate targets for an impulse move but prices retrace as often from such levels as cross them (*see* Figure 9.1). Furthermore, the viability of the system given in this book is not dependent on targets; exiting at a trailing stop loss is quite sufficient. This has the added advantage of making the system wholly mechanical. It is a known fact that some subjectivity is always introduced when targets are calculated in any particular manner. This may result in unnecessary confusion, thus jeopardizing the profitability of the system itself.

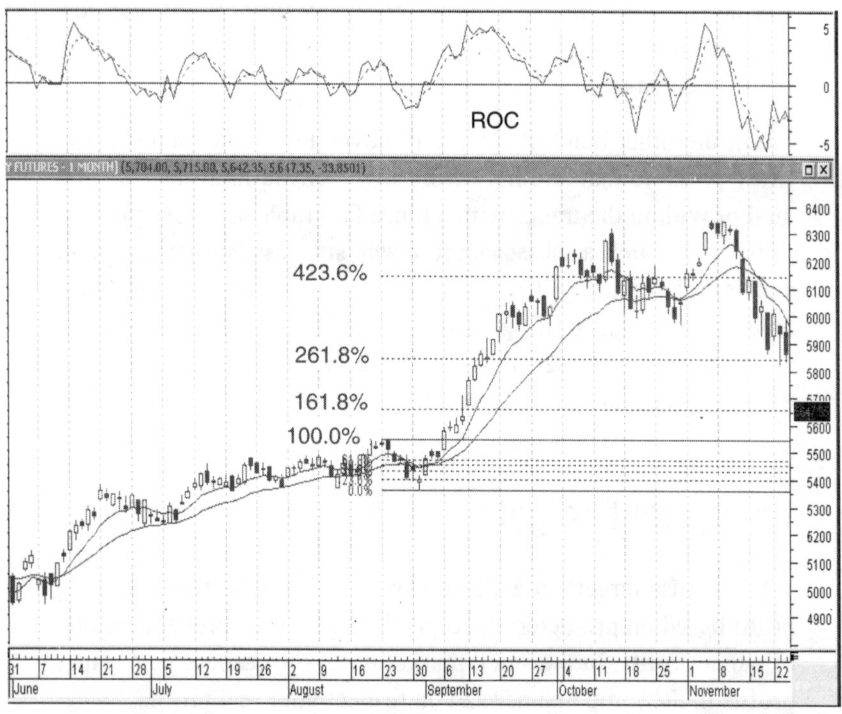

Figure 9.1: **Chart showing the method of calculating Fibonacci targets**

Another important point to understand is that when most of the trading is done with the trend, 2.618 targets are more likely to be achieved.

Alternatively, once the target is achieved, the trader can look at one degree lower time frame for an opposing signal to exit half of his position.

For more details regarding the use of targets, the reader is advised to go through Tony Plummer's book, *The Psychology of Technical Analysis.*

~

10

~

Money Management and Position Sizing

Money Management

Money management addresses the questions of how much money you can afford to lose in any single trade.

Traders are often told that no more than 2% of one's capital should be risked on any single trade and that you should not hold more than 5 ongoing trades at any one time. In this manner, a maximum of only 10% of your capital is at risk at any moment.

The reasoning behind this approach is that in this manner you can diversify your trading portfolio and use your trading capital to its maximum potential. But the problem is that if you are totally new to the stock markets — or even if you have had some past experience of the markets but you trade without sound methodology, then you must consider yourself a new trader — you would like to tread carefully. Furthermore, you are still learning the ropes and would like to trade within limits, but soundly. Hence, initially it may be a good idea to trade only

Nifty futures, and then diversify elsewhere as your capital builds up.

Consider, for example, that the capital available with the trader is ₹10 lakh. He can, therefore, risk 2% of this amount, i.e. ₹20,000 on any given trade. He decides to take a trade in Nifty. His entry point with Nifty is at 10,000 and his estimated stop loss is at 9,900, a difference of 100 points. He may decide to buy 200 Nifty so that his maximum loss would not be more than ₹20,000. But the total cost of 200 Nifty at 10,000 levels is ₹20 lakh. For a trade of this size, he may be required to deposit a margin of ₹2 lakh with the broker (the margin requirement of exchanges keeps on changing and is usually between 10% to 15%). What will he do with the remaining ₹8 lakh of his capital? The only way to use this capital is to diversify into 5 items.

If, on the other hand, the trader was to risk 10% of his capital on a single Nifty trade rather than risking 2% of capital each on five different trades and thus is able to utilize all his capital in Nifty alone, then even a string of 10 continuous losses — which is not as rare as you may think — will put him out of business. None of the statistically proven profitable systems can guarantee that there wouldn't be a string of losses. However, if the trader is having capital to trade even after such a losing string, he is guaranteed to make good his losses as well as earn some more. Risking 10% of one's capital on any single trade is like committing financial suicide. Systems need time and capital to become perfect and to perform.

Before we go any further, it also needs emphasizing that the capital requirement is dependent on the position size which is sought to be entered — which, in turn, is dependent upon the trading system and the time frame being traded. Thus, for example, it is possible to trade with much smaller capital using 15-minute charts as compared to daily charts. Furthermore, while a trader would have lower capital in the beginning of his career, he may be in a position to meet the additional requirements —

mark-to-market losses — from his salary or business income. The trader must be comfortable with the risk being assumed in each trade otherwise the element of fear will hinder trading as per the requirement of the system. A loss of ₹20,000 on a capital of ₹10 lakh is only 2% and can easily be recovered by a profitable trade but a loss of ₹1 lakh on a capital of ₹10 lakh can be mentally devastating and may even result in cessation of trading altogether. Hence, the losses should be kept to a minimum with proper diversification.

The question of money management is also related to the following factors.

Your Capacity to Bear Losses

One's capacity to bear losses will decide the time frame that one should be trading. If one wants to go at it slowly, one may choose the daily time frame. An hourly time frame may give ten trades in approximately 2 to 3 months whereas a daily time frame using the same system will provide a similar number of trades in perhaps one year. Therefore, traders using hourly charts should take lower risk as compared to those using daily charts. If the risk per trade on daily time frame is ₹20,000, then a risk of ₹10,000 on hourly time frame, and a risk of ₹5,000 on 15-minute time frame is adequate.

How Much Money You Want to Make in a Certain Period

A trader should not assume special powers attached to any system until he has proved it to himself in real time. Howsoever logical and profitable a system may appear — or whosoever may be selling it to you, including this author — the trader should always assume a success rate of no more than 50%, and that, too, with a lot of skepticism. You also need to verify that the winning trades have the capacity to provide you with bigger gains than there are losses from losing trades. The trader should be able to determine the profitability of the system after approximately 100 trades done in real time. This figure needs to be worked out as profit per trade on a given risk amount.

Suppose the risk taken on each trade was ₹10,000 and after 100 trades the net profit is ₹5,00,000, then the profit per trade is ₹5,000 (₹5,00,000 divided by the total number of trades, i.e. 100).

Another thing which needs to be determined is the approximate likely frequency of trading signals.

Let's suppose one gets about 50 signals in a year — quite likely, if one is using the hourly time frame and trading in 5 securities simultaneously. Now, we know that the trader stands to make 50 x 5,000 = ₹2,50,000 in a year's time if he risks ₹10,000 on a single trade. If he wants to earn ₹10 lakh in a year's time, then he is required to takc a risk of at least ₹40,000 per trade and should therefore have a minimum capital of ₹20 lakh which will enable him to trade in 5 different securities. This amount will be sufficient to meet any margin requirement as well as day to day losses.

In case you intend to trade using the daily time frame, then you may get only ten signals in a year and, commensurately, you will have to take much higher risk on each trade to make the same amount of money.

Your Dependence on Trading Income

Since fewer signals are generated in daily time frame, there can be long periods when you are not able to make any profits. An intraday time frame (15 minutes to 60 minutes) will be decidedly more suitable for a trader who is trying to earn his day-to-day living expenses from his trading income. Smaller capital may, however, be adequate for trading in smaller time frame charts.

The Time You Have for Trading

If the trader cannot devote any time during the day for analyzing the markets, then he is better off trading on the daily time frame although his profits are likely to be lower with the same amount of risk, as compared to trading with intraday time frames. In case the trader's experience suggests that he may become a full time trader rather than work for anything else then he may decide to change to intraday time frame from the daily time frame.

Position Sizing

Position sizing refers to the size of the trade you should put in place once you get an entry signal from your system.

Strategies of Position Sizing

An **equal rupee strategy** would mean that you are going to buy (or sell) shares whose total value is a fixed amount in terms of rupees. For example, if you decide that your trade size is a constant ₹10 lakh, then you will buy 200 shares of Nifty if the Nifty level is 5,000, or 100 shares if the level is 10,000, and so on.

An **equal number strategy** requires you to buy a fixed number of shares, whatever may be the market price of each share. For example, you might decide to buy 200 shares irrespective of the price being 5,000 or 10,000.

An **equal risk strategy** means that the trader is limiting his loss per trade to a fixed amount of money. For example, if the risk to be taken on every trade is limited to ₹10,000, then the trader will buy 100 shares if the stop loss is 100 points away, and will buy 200 shares if the stop loss is 50 points away.

Which of these is better? In an exhaustive study, Van K. Tharp in his book *Trade Your Way to Financial Freedom* has conclusively shown that the equal risk strategy is far superior as compared to the other two strategies not only in terms of bigger profits but also in controlling risk. Furthermore, the other two strategies have the propensity of giving unexpected losses and we must remember that the only things under our control are our capital and emotions. The other things are controlled by the market, of which we are the slaves. We must try to eliminate as many unpredictable items from our trading as possible.

~

We have now clearly laid down the principles you need to follow for money management and position sizing. These rules apply to trading in any single security say, for example, Nifty futures. If you intend to trade in other securities as well then you will need commensurately larger funds to start with. But remember never to trade in more than five securities at any one time since this will seriously jeopardize your trading success. As you become a more accomplished trader, you can start trading bigger positions but do not increase the number of securities being traded at any one time, or the frequency of your trades. Technically, it may sound easy to trade in ten securities but, ultimately, this kind of trading will drain you emotionally, with deleterious outcome on health and finances.

Summary of Money Management and Position Sizing Rules

1. Do not risk more than 2% of your capital on any single trade.
2. Reduce the per trade risk to 1% if trading on the basis of hourly charts, and to 0.5% if trading on the basis of 15-minute charts.

3. Trading in daily charts cannot be dependent upon to provide regular income and the trader must use smaller time frame charts if regular income is desired.
4. Traders using hourly or 15-minute charts must watch the market during the period it is open
5. Do not trade in more than 5 securities at any one time.
6. For position sizing, equal risk strategy is better than equal rupee strategy or equal share strategy
7. Keep expectations low and make a realistic calculation of expected profits and losses

~

11

~

Drawdowns and Profits

Drawdown means loss. Profit means money, which means freedom, holidays, better life style, etc.

In an excellent discussion on the subject of emotions in trading in his book *The Psychology of Technical Analysis*, Tony Plummer has pointed out that human mind is conditioned to look at a loss as a sort of blot on one's personal ego and not just as a logical factor of the trading environment. If there were no losses or drawdowns then everybody would be a great trader. Remember that it is not your capacity to understand this or some other book, nor your capacity to open an account with the broker, nor your capacity to arrange capital for trading, nor your competency with the technical analysis software that will determine your success or failure as a trader. It is the ability to face drawdowns and yet be able to continue trading that is the hall mark of a successful trader.

The ability to bear sustained periods of drawdowns is the single most important hallmark of a successful trader. No one can rise to great heights unless he has learned to fall gracefully, and without debilitating injury.

A proven trading system can help in this because the trader will at least have the confidence of getting into profitable trades after the drawdown ends. No matter how successful a trader may become, there will always be drawdowns.

The discipline to keep on using the same system despite drawdowns is very important, especially if you have been using the system for some time and have faith in it. All systems work for some time; equally, all systems fail some times. It is possible that when your system is losing money, some other system is making profits. For example, if your system makes money when a trend is in force, it is unlikely to make money in a sideways market. During sideways markets, when you are suffering from a period of drawdowns, then some other trader using a different system, one which is more suitable for sideways markets, may be making profits. But this should, in no case, prompt you to abandon your own tested system and try a new one. A new system should be used only when it has proved itself to be better than the previous one.

When to Increase Risk

A trader often overestimates his capacity to bear drawdowns. This overestimation may in part be due to the fact that the trader feels himself lucky or intelligent and concludes that he will somehow be able to minimize the losses, or that he may even be able to avoid them completely. This will only make him a poor trader. Every trader needs to recognize that one cannot control or influence the market's direction and that a stop loss which is not capable of tackling market noise will only result in his getting thrown out of some very good trades. The previous estimates of drawdowns, based on research and experience, should never be reduced and the trader should never create a larger position in the market merely because he now feels more confident.

The ability to accumulate profits, on the other hand, is often underestimated. A trader may start with the assumption that he wants to make only a small amount of money from trading but even a few profitable trades in succession immediately make him start dreaming big. But profits will not become bigger just to please your ego, nor will losses evaporate overnight to prove that you are lucky.

A well thought out plan, however, can accomplish the same goal if applied in a disciplined manner. Suppose you have made a profit of ₹2,50,000 by trading Nifty futures, assuming a risk of ₹10,000 per trade and taking a total of 50 trades and would now like to make higher profits in your next trades. Before working out a profit figure, first ask yourself how much you are willing to lose. Remember that you are still taking a total risk of ₹1 lakh on 10 trades, as per your previous risk level of ₹10,000 per trade. Now suppose you are prepared to lose ₹1.50 lakh in your next ten trades, then do not take more than ₹15,000 risk per trade. This way you will still be left with ₹1 lakh of accumulated profits, out of the total profit of ₹2.50 lakh you made before.

The other approach, not recommended, is that of deciding expected profits first. Perhaps you would like to make ₹5 lakh profit. For that, you would need to increase your per trade risk to ₹20,000. Now suppose that you get a string of 10 straight losses. You would lose ₹2 lakh, leaving you with only ₹50,000 of net profits, whereupon you may be tempted to blame the system and may give it up prematurely.

It is very important for a trader's well being that he must strive to maintain a positive balance sheet at all times.

~

12

~

Some Details for Novice Traders

This chapter contains some points regarding stock market trading which may be skipped by those already conversant with market concepts and terminology.

Long Position

A long position means owning some equity, bond or commodity, or having the right to own an underlying security at some future date. When an investor buys a stock from his broker with the idea of selling it later to generate profit, he is said to be long on that stock. He is also the owner of the stock till the time he sells it. Similarly when a trader buys a futures contract, he "owns" the right to buy the underlying shares at any time before the expiry date and is therefore said to be holding a long position till he sells his "right," namely the ownership of the futures contract, to someone else.

Short Position

A short position means a trader sells a security — equity, bond or commodity — without being its owner. For example, if he sells shares of a company, he is obliged to deliver those shares before a predetermined date, namely the expiry date of the contract. Now, in order meet this obligation he will have to buy those shares from the market. This is irrespective of the fact whether the prices have fallen during the period, in which case it would be beneficial for the trader having the short position, or have risen in which case it is harmful for the trader having the short position.

I have often found it very difficult to explain the concept of short position to people other than futures traders who always seem to know about it. The very idea of being able to sell something which is not owned is alien to most people. **But the concept of short selling is extremely important because a trader who has learnt the art of short selling will not be sitting idle when the markets are falling but would instead be profiting from them.**

Let us consider an example.

Suppose you sell 1,000 shares of Reliance Industries (as one contract of Reliance futures) through your broker at a price of ₹1,100 per share for a total value of ₹11,00,000. After a few days, but before the expiry date of the contract which in India is the last Thursday of the month, you find that the price per share is now only ₹900. You ask your broker to exit your sell position. The broker does so by buying one contract of Reliance from the market at a price of ₹900 each for a total value of ₹9,00,000. In this process, you have gained a net profit of ₹2,00,000 (₹11,00,000 – 9,00,000). On the other hand, had the price increased to ₹1,300, you would then have lost ₹2,00,000 on your short position.

It should also be noted that whereas a long position can be created in the cash market by taking delivery of the stock by making full payment, and also in the futures market by paying a margin to the broker, **a short position cannot be created in the cash market — unless you square it off before the market closes on the day of the sale itself — and can only be created in the futures market.**

Cash Market

This is that segment of the Indian stock exchanges (NSE and BSE) where shares are bought and sold against full payment. For example, if you want to buy 300 shares of Reliance at a price of ₹1,000 each, then you will have to pay ₹3 lakh to the broker to get the shares deposited in your demat account. If, instead, you sell the same number of shares then you are entitled to receive ₹3 lakh from the broker. In the cash market, you can buy and sell even a single share if you wish.

Futures Market

This is another segment of the stock markets where the rules are different as compared to the cash market. In the futures market, a trader has to buy and sell shares in pre-defined lots, called contracts. For example, you would have had to buy, or sell, a minimum of 500 shares (equivalent to one contract) of Reliance Industries as one lot and then you can buy or sell in multiples of 500 shares only, i.e. 500, 1,000, 1,500, 2,000 shares, and so on. Besides, only a limited number of stocks* are traded in the Indian futures market as compared to more than 5,000 stocks in the cash

---

* Approximately 175 at the time of writing in 2018.

segment of BSE*. In India, the futures contracts expire on the last Thursday of the month. Also, it is not wise to buy far month contracts as they may be quite illiquid and exiting them may be a problem.

Despite these limitations, the futures market offers the following big advantages:

1. A trader can have a long position as well as a short position in the futures market. In the cash segment, on the other hand, long positions can be held for as long as one wants but a short position must be squared by market close.

2. Only a small amount of money (approximately 10% to 25%) has to be paid to the broker as margin money for trading futures. Thus, in order to buy a contract of Nifty futures worth approximately ₹7.5 lakh, an amount of only ₹1 lakh would be required whereas a similar transaction in cash segment would require the full amount of ₹7.5 lakh to be paid.

3. The brokerage in futures market is miniscule as compared to the cash market. The brokerage may be approximately ₹60 on purchase and sale of futures contract worth ₹10 lakh whereas the same may be as much ₹1,500 for a similar transaction in the cash market.

4. STT (Security Transaction Tax) is much lower in the futures market as compared to the cash market. STT in cash market is 0.1% and is charged on both buy and sell transactions whereas STT in the futures market is only 0.01% and charged only on the sell side. For example, STT on purchase and sale of shares worth ₹10 lakh will be ₹2,000 whereas the same will only be ₹100 in the futures market.

---

* Up-to-date information on the number of stocks listed and their contract sizes in the futures market is available on the websites of the two premier Indian exchanges — www.bseindia.com and www.nseindia.com.

The only problem is that in case you wish to take your position into the next month, you have to exit your existing position prior to the market closure on the last Thursday of the month, and buy a new contract for the next month. The new contract will be available at a slight premium to account for the interest rates. This process is known as "roll over."

Options

Options are a totally different kettle of fish and are not covered in this book. Several excellent books are already available on the subject. Suffice it to say that it is very difficult to apply the technical tools described in this book to options analysis and those who are interested in trading options should remember that there is no such thing as a free lunch. Every trading instrument has its own risk and reward ratio and dealing in options should only be attempted after having acquired a thorough knowledge of the subject.

~

Part 3

~

The Fearless Trading System

13
~
Mechanical Swings

A swing is nothing but tops and bottoms, or pivots, which are placed clearly apart from one another on the chart. But can there be a mechanical way of determining swings?

In this book, I am presenting a totally new way of looking at swings. I have devised this method by using price rate of change (ROC) which is a momentum indicator just like RSI or Stochastic. The ROC calculation compares the percentage change in current price with the price "n" periods ago and this is then plotted as a graph. The mechanical swing is plotted as given below:

- First, a 5-period price ROC is plotted on a chart.
- Then a 3-period exponential moving average of ROC is plotted as a dotted line on the same chart.
- A **swing high** is the highest price when the dotted line is above the zero line.
- A **swing low** is the lowest price when the dotted line is below the zero line.
- A **swing breakout** means that a swing high (Point A) is followed by a swing low (Point B) and the price thereafter crosses the swing high formed at Point A on the upside.

- A long trade entry is made by planning a buy stop loss at the swing high (Point A).
- A short trade entry is made by planning a sell stop loss at the swing low (Point B).

We will explain all these points as we go along.

Calculating ROC

The 5-period ROC is calculated as follows:

$$\text{5-Period ROC} = \frac{\text{Price Today} - \text{Price of 5 days ago}}{\text{Price of 5 days ago}} \times 100$$

As an example, consider Table 13.1.

Table 13.1

Calculating 5-Day ROC

Day	*Price (₹)*	*5-day ROC*
1	500	-
2	508	-
3	510	-
4	515	-
5	510	-
6	495	-1
7	508	0
8	526	3.13
9	528	2.52
10	540	5.88

The beauty of using the 5-period ROC along with a 3-period exponential moving average is that it provides a mechanical way of determining swings. Not only does this help to avoid the errors in determining swings on the basis of visual inspection, it also helps to avoid many whipsaws when the 5-period ROC swing is used without its 3-period EMA.

An 8-day EMA (exponential moving average) line and 21-day EMA line, respectively, are shown in the daily chart of Nifty futures in Figure 13.1. A price ROC indicator of 5-periods is also shown in the upper panel of the same chart which shows several swing highs and swing lows. On 22 January 2010, the 8-day EMA line crossed below the 21-day EMA line. Since the trend as per the weekly chart was up at this time, this would be considered as a correction in the uptrend and the trader should ready himself to make an entry into the buy side, i.e. get ready to make a long entry.

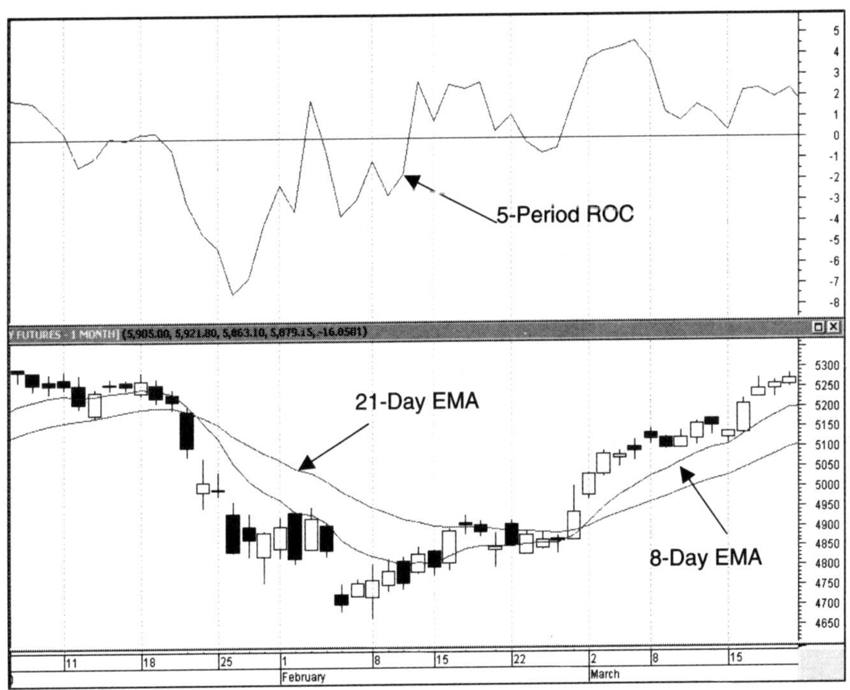

Figure 13.1: **Daily chart of Nifty futures, with ROC plotted in the upper panel**

~

Let me illustrate as to how the use of a 3-period moving average superimposed on a 5-period ROC helps to avoid whipsaws.

The magnified chart in Figure 13.2 covers the sub-period from 7 January 2010 to 21 January 2010. A 5-day ROC is shown, along with a 3-period exponential moving average (mechanical swing) in the upper panel of the chart. On 14 January, the 5-day ROC went above the zero line, and then fell below the zero line on 15 January. If only the 5-day ROC is used to determine swings, then the trader would have positioned himself to go long at the 14 January high — which would have resulted in loss. However, due to super-imposition of the 3-day moving average

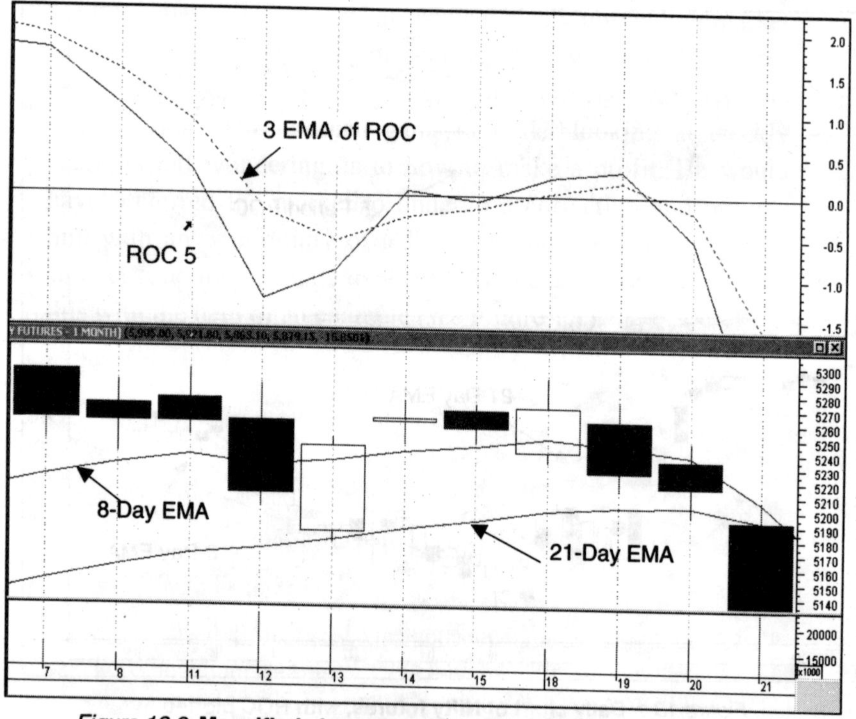

Figure 13.2: **Magnified chart of a portion of the time period covered in Figure 13.2**

~

of ROC on the 5-day ROC, the trader would have positioned to go long only when the high of 18 January was crossed. Since the high of 18 January was not crossed by the subsequent price action, this potential trade was avoided due to the use of 5-day ROC in combination with its own 3-day moving average. The trade was finally entered on 26 February as shown in Figure 13.3.

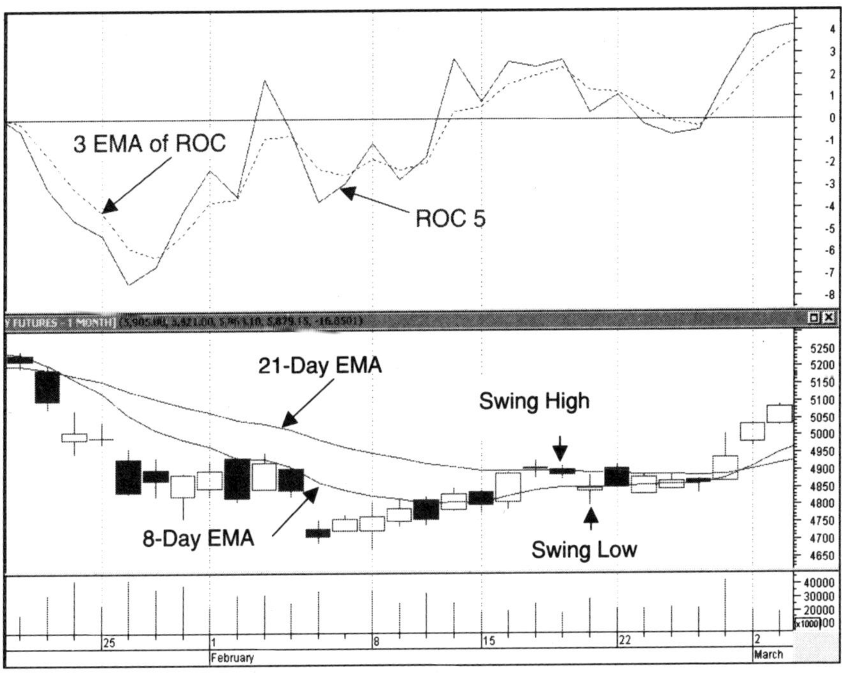

Figure 13.3: **In this daily chart of Nifty futures covering the period from 22 January 2010 to 3 March 2010, a swing high was created by ROC on 17 February followed by a swing low on 19 February 2010 (price made a low on 19 February while the mechanical swing went below the zero line on 25 February), enabling a long entry on 26 February when the price broke out from the previous swing high of 4,928 established on 17 February 2010.**

~

The great advantage of using mechanical swings, as I prefer to call them, is that the signals generated by them cannot be misinterpreted. Even if the signal gives a loss, a trader has the confidence that he has not erred in implementing his system. In general, however, and in my personal experience, trading on the basis of mechanical swings generates consistent, solid profits in the long term.

~

14

~

Parameters of the Fearless Trading System

Price Chart

Prices can be depicted in many ways by charting software. The line method is not suitable for our system as it shows only the closing prices while our system requires buy signals to be taken only when a previous swing high is broken.

The choice then is between bars and candlesticks.

As you can see in Figure 14.1, in a candlestick chart each candle shows the opening price, the closing price, the highest price and the lowest price for the period the candle represents. The blank (or white) candles are those where the price closed higher than the previous candle's closing price, and the black (or filled) candles are those where the price closed lower than the closing price of the previous candle. The candles may also be shown in color; for example, generally blue or green candles

Figure 14.1: **A price chart in the form of candlesticks**

~

being the up candles and red candles being down candles. Furthermore, in up candles the opening price forms the lower boundary of the candle's body, the closing price forms the upper boundary, the highest price of the period is the upper wick, and the lowest part of the period is depicted by the lower wick.

Figure 14.2: **A Price chart in the form of bars**

~

I am used to candlesticks but if you prefer, you can even use bars which are shown in Figure 14.2.

Determining the Trend on the Higher Time Frame Chart

For a trader desirous of trading in the daily time frame, namely on the basis of the daily chart and not on intraday basis, it is profitable to first ascertain the direction of the longer term trend as shown by the weekly chart.

Correspondingly, the direction of the trend in the daily chart is important if the trading signals are to be taken in the hourly time frame. Remember, one of the best, and proven, tenets of technical analysis is that a trend once established is likely to continue until there is sufficient evidence that a reversal has occurred. Furthermore, there are well defined patterns which are likely to occur at turning points and the trading system being propounded in this book will generally help you to be on the right side of the market when such an event does take place.

A trend can be determined in the following manner:

1. Through visual inspection (*see* Figure 14.3);
2. By using trend lines (*see* Figure 14.4); and
3. By using moving averages (*see* Figure 14.5).

Due to my desire to keep the system completely mechanical in nature, I have chosen moving averages as the preferred indicator. Visual inspection and trend lines are not only subjective but also require considerable experience.

A simple moving average (SMA) is the average price over a fixed period of days. It is called a moving average as its value changes with time. Suppose an 8-day moving average is to be calculated from 1 January, and assuming there are no trading holidays in between, then the eight closing prices from 1 January to 8 January will be summed up and divided by 8. This will give us a simple moving average of 8 days, as on 8 January. To calculate its value for 9 January, we shall drop the closing price of 1 January and add the closing price of 9 January and then divide the sum by 8. This will give us a simple moving average of 8 days as on 9 January. And, so on.

While a simple moving average gives equal weight to all data, an exponential moving average (EMA) gives more weight to recent prices and lesser weight to the earlier ones. Exponential moving averages are generally better but acceptable results can also be obtained by using simple moving averages.

Nowadays, all the above calculations are conveniently performed automatically by computers and are better left to them.

Figure 14.3: **Weekly chart of Nifty showing an uptrend from March 2009 onwards. At what stage can you say by visual inspection that the trend has turned upward?**

~

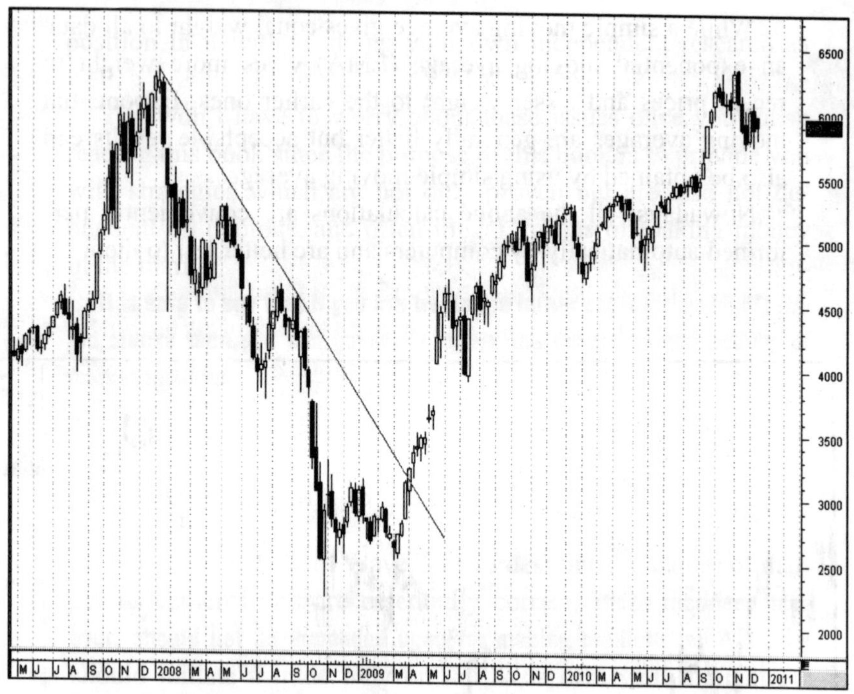

Figure 14.4: **Weekly chart of Nifty showing a trend line drawn from the January 2008 top but the trend line appears too steep and its break would have been considered invalid if the rules of trend line breaks were strictly adhered to. Interested reader will find rules for drawing valid trend lines and their breaks in Chapter 26.**

~

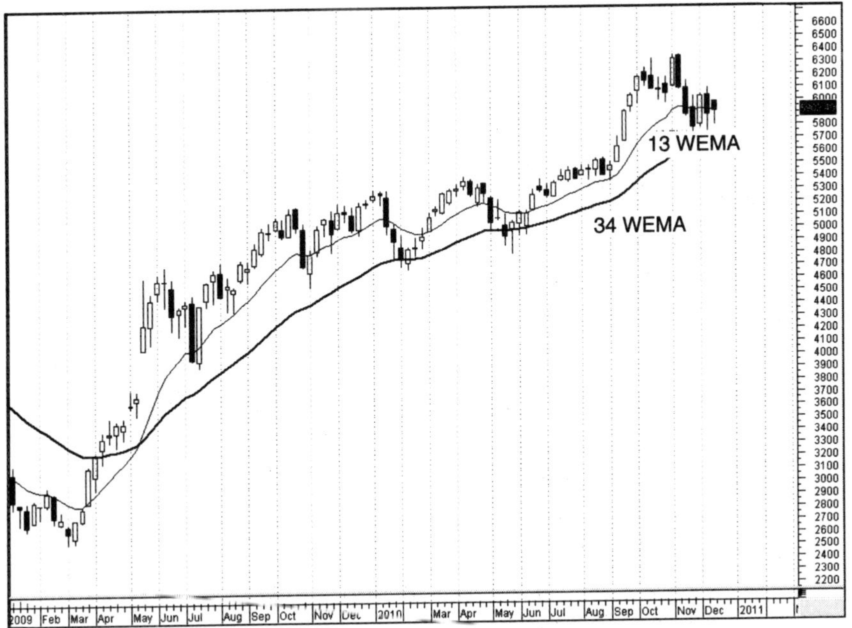

Figure 14.5: **On 22 May 2009, the 13-week exponential moving average (13WEMA) line crossed above the 34-week exponential moving average (34WEMA) line when the trend turned up. Nifty was still in an uptrend in December 2010, where this chart ends. The 13WEMA line crossed below 34WEMA line in March 2011 when this uptrend can be said to have ended as per our system.**

~

My research and experience suggest that **a combination of 13WMA (weekly moving average) and 34WMA is capable of determining the major trend adequately for our purpose**. Shorter moving averages, such as 5WMA and 8WMA combinations will behave more or less like the weekly MACD and are therefore not suitable for the system presented in this book. Longer moving averages will take more time to turn up or down, thereby preventing an opportunity for an early entry in the newly developing trend. However, it is my opinion that most combinations of moving averages work adequately depending upon the entry and exit criteria. **Please, however, keep in mind that I am not advocating entries based on moving average crossovers.**

So, for trading on the basis of daily charts, the higher level trend is considered up for our trading system if the 13WMA line is above the 34WMA line and is considered down if the 13WMA line is below the 34WMA line.

Use of Daily MACD (Moving Average Convergence Divergence)

Originally developed by Gerald Appel in the US, MACD is a very popular momentum indicator.

First, two exponential moving averages, namely those of 12 periods and 26 periods are calculated. The difference between the two — the 12-period EMA and 26-period EMA — is plotted on a graph as a solid line, which is also known as the MACD line. This line oscillates below and above the zero (equilibrium) line.

Second, a 9-period exponential moving average of the MACD line is calculated and plotted as a dotted line. This is known as the signal line. A buy signal is generated by this indicator when the MACD line crosses the signal line from below and goes above it — and *vice versa* for sell signals.

The beauty of MACD is that it provides the earliest indication of a changing trend. For example, if the trend in the weekly chart is up, namely the 13WMA line is above the 34WMA line, and prices are rising, then the daily MACD is likely to be in buy mode as well. If the price now starts moving sideways or starts

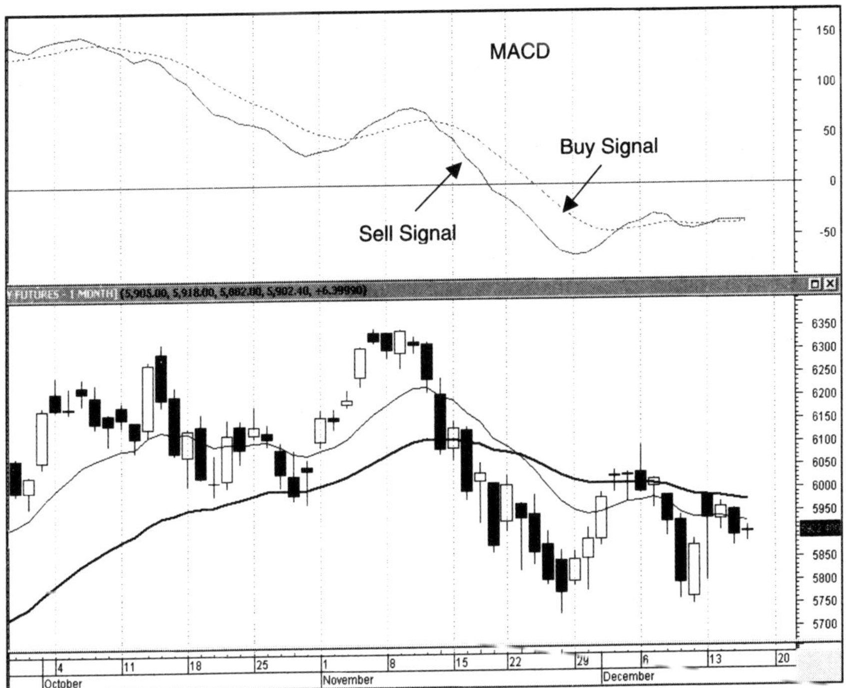

Figure 14.6: **Weekly chart of Nifty futures showing the MACD graph in the upper panel. A buy signal is generated when the solid line crosses the dotted line on the upside and a sell signal is generated in the opposite manner. A horizontal line drawn in the center is the zero line.**

~

to fall, the daily MACD will be the first indicator to move into sell mode even though the 8DMA line would still be above the 21DMA line. Once the daily MACD gives a sell signal, either a minor correction of the uptrend in weekly chart may take place, or it may be the beginning of a downtrend in the weekly chart (*see* Figure 14.6).

On such occasions, the first task for the trader should be to exit all long positions by appropriately tightening the stop losses.

Second, he should now let the market correct and wait for another buy signal in the direction of the uptrend on the weekly chart.

Third, the trader could also use the opportunity for short selling which will give him huge profits if it happens to be the beginning of a downtrend in the weekly chart.

A caveat is again in order here. Short selling and exiting long position are not to be done automatically when the daily MACD gives a sell signal but only when certain other conditions are also fulfilled, as explained in Chapter 15.

I do not place much importance to buy and sell signals generated by MACD but use it merely as one of the tools to determine entry levels.

8DMA and 21DMA Crossovers

Now that we have described the method of determining the trend on the higher time frame, i.e. on the weekly chart, the trader should focus on the daily chart. Here, you are looking for an opportunity to make an entry in the direction of the trend in the weekly chart.

If, for example, the trend in the weekly chart is up, you would like to see some correction on the daily chart before contemplating a long position. This can be done by using various methods, such as RSI (*see* Figure 14.7), Stochastic (*see* Figure 14.8) or moving averages, etc. Again, I have given preference to moving average combinations due to ease of interpretation. Suppose a trader goes for RSI instead, he will have to choose a period for RSI (5, 7, 9, 12 or 14, etc.) and then also set the upper and lower limits for overbought (60 or 70) and oversold levels (30 or 40). Now suppose that his oversold limit is at 40 and the RSI this time corrects only up to 40.2 levels. Should he then buy on a

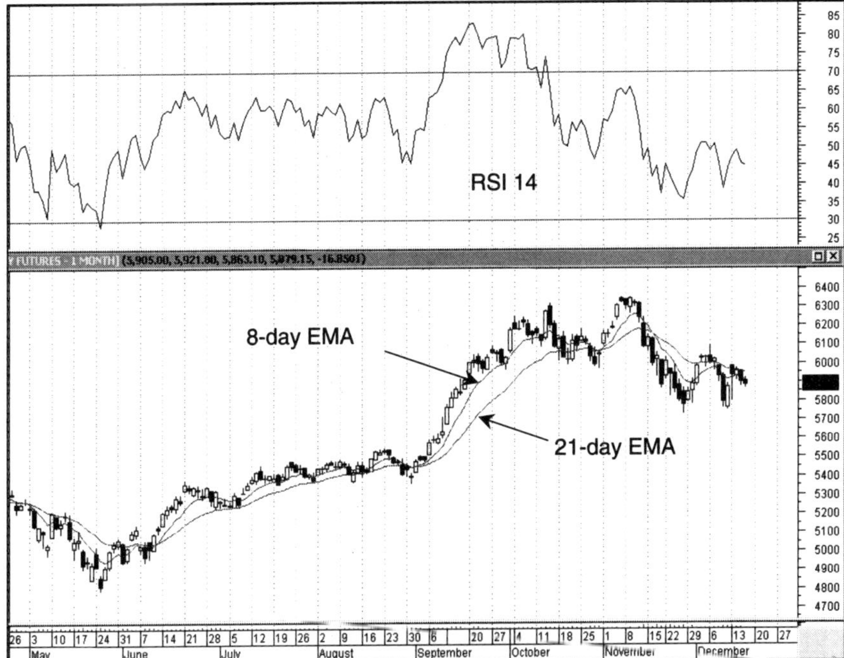

Figure 14.7: **The 8-day EMA and 21-day EMA lines are shown in this chart. RSI 14 days is shown in the panel above the price chart. To get an oversold reading in RSI 14, you would need to modify the criteria for oversold RSI and set it at 40, or you may shorten the RSI period to 9 days. However, once the 8-day EMA line goes below 21-day EMA line, It permits you to plan your entry into a long position since the trend on the weekly chart is still up.**

~

swing breakout or ignore it? The use of 8DMA and 21DMA line crossovers, on the other hand, will not only catch most of the meaningful trade entry opportunities but will also prevent any confusion regarding the magnitude of correction. Furthermore, oscillators such as RSI and Stochastic can go into oversold territory even if the price moves sideways. This is because these are momentum indicators. Moving averages, on the other hand, are trend indicators and the shorter term moving average will not cross the longer term moving average downward until the prices themselves have started to correct. **We would like to make an entry in the direction of the uptrend in the weekly chart only after confirming a downtrend in the daily time frame.**

If the 13WMA line is above the 34WMA line, then the trader is looking for the 8DMA line to go below the 21DMA line to plan his entry into a long position — and *vice versa* for short positions.

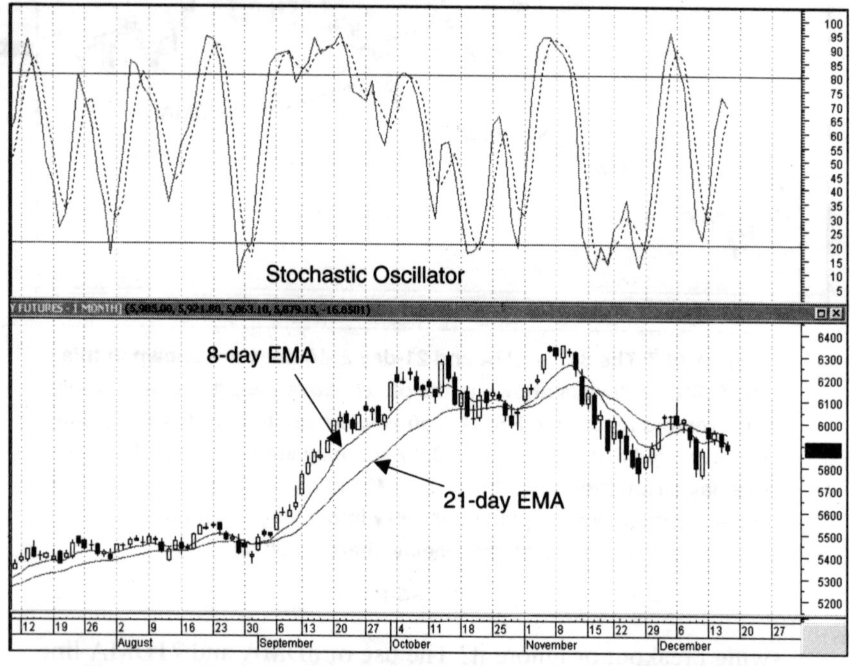

Figure 14.8: **This chart shows the 8-day EMA and 21-day EMA lines in the lower panel. The Stochastic oscillator (5, 3) is shown in the panel above the price chart. There are systems using the Stochastic but this oscillator is not suitable for application in the system being described in this book.**

~

The mechanical swing has already been described in an earlier chapter and this, more or less, completes the armory of technical tools that we need.

~

15

~

Rules of the Fearless Trading System

The system being presented in this book has been used by the author for more than last 15 years with a high degree of success. However, there is always scope for innovations and you should certainly be able to add more value after some experience.

When 13WMA is Above 34WMA

This means that the trend shown by the weekly chart is up. The following signals are to be taken even if the 13WMA line is falling, so long as it is still above the 34WMA line, since any significant correction enabling us to enter on the basis of the daily chart is likely to also make the 13WMA line fall a little bit. The reverse is true when the trend on the weekly chart is down.

Pro-Trend Buy Trade

- Buy when a swing breakout occurs on the daily chart while the 8DMA line is below the 21DMA line.
- The initial stop loss should be set at the most recent swing low.
- Exit when the initial, or trailing, stop loss is hit, as the case may be.

As already explained in Chapter 10, full risk, i.e. up to 2% of the total trading capital, can be taken in such a trade as this is a pro-trend trade with a higher probability of being profitable.

Contra-Trend Sell Trade

- Sell when the daily MACD goes into sell mode, and the 8DMA line is still above the 21 DMA line, and a swing breakdown takes place on the daily chart.
- Set the initial stop loss at the most recent swing high.
- Exit when the initial or trailing stop loss, as the case may be, is hit.

In such a case, only half the usual risk, i.e. up to 1% of capital, is to be taken since this is a contra-trend trade with a lower probability of success. However, losses in this kind of trades are likely to be offset by the system's occasional big profits and, overall, these trades deliver positive returns, if undertaken repeatedly.

Reversal Trades

- If the stop loss is hit on a short position, i.e. in a sell trade, while the 8DMA line is still above the 21DMA line, then exiting the short position also requires simultaneously going long with half the usual risk, i.e. with a risk of 1% of the capital.

- On the other hand, if the 8DMA line has gone below the 21DMA line, then exiting a short position should be followed by simultaneously going long with full risk (2% of the capital) as per the pro-trend buy signal explained above.

When 13WMA is Below 34WMA

In this case, the trend as per the weekly time frame is down.

Pro-Trend Sell Trade

- Sell when a swing breakdown occurs on the daily chart while the 8DMA line is above the 21DMA line.
- Set the initial stop loss at the most recent swing high. Exit when the initial or trailing stop loss is hit.
- Full risk (2% of the capital) is taken as this is a pro-trend trade with a higher probability of profits.

Contra-Trend Buy Trade

- Buy when the daily MACD goes into buy mode and a swing breakout takes place on the daily chart, while the 8DMA line is still below the 21DMA line.
- Set the initial stop loss at the most recent swing low.
- Exit when the initial, or trailing, stop loss is hit.
- Half the usual risk is to be taken (1% of the capital) since this is a contra-trend trade with a relatively lower probability of success.

Reversal Trades

- If the stop loss is hit on the long position while the 8DMA line is still below the 21DMA line, then besides exiting the long position, you should also go short with half the usual risk (1% of the capital).
- If the 8DMA line has gone above the 21DMA line, then exiting the long position should be followed by simultaneously going short with full risk (2% of the capital) as per the pro-trend sell signal explained above.

~

In Chapter 16, we shall explain the rationale behind the system. With minor modifications, the system can be used for short term trading as well. While a trade taken on the basis of daily charts may last a few weeks to a few months, the trade taken with same strategy on 15-minutes charts may last for only 1 to 3 days. But, remember, smaller the time frame used, more is the trader's involvement. Thus, while a trader using daily charts need not watch the market at all during trading hours, those using a 15-minute chart will find it impossible to stay away from the trading platform. Hence, short term trading is more like a regular job while medium term trading based on daily charts provides extra income to those holding a regular job elsewhere.

~

16

~

Why the Fearless Trading System Works

The Pro-Trend Trade

Our pro-trend signal — say, the buy signal during an uptrend on the weekly chart — is simply an attempt to enter a long position after a correction.

In other words, we enter when the longer term trend is up, which is signaled by the 13WMA line being above the 34WMA line in the weekly chart, and the shorter trend, as seen on daily charts, is down — the 8DMA line is below the 21DMA line — thereby signaling an oversold situation.

A long position created at such a time provides the maximum possibility of gain with only a small possibility of loss. This is so because we enter the trade when the price breaks out of a mechanical swing. It is also advisable to take on full risk (2% of the capital) in a pro-trend trade due to a higher probability of the trade being profitable.

The Contra-Trend Trade

The contra-trend trade — the sell trade when the longer trend signaled by the weekly chart is up — is a minor modification of the system propounded by Alexander Elder in his famous book, *Trading for a Living.*

We take a contra-trend trade when:

- The long term trend is up, indicated by the 13WMA line being above the 34WMA line.
- Daily MACD has just gone into the sell mode, suggesting that the market may be entering into a correction from a longer term overbought level.
- It is also possible that daily MACD sell signal is a whipsaw since the uptrend in the weekly chart is still intact. It would certainly not be advisable to sell on the basis of the daily MACD sell signal alone. It is the market action which takes place after the daily MACD goes into the sell mode that will decide whether to short sell or not.

As will be shown in the chapters that follow, the mechanical swing based on ROC will also move below the zero line as soon as the daily MACD goes into sell mode. Thereafter, if this swing low (Point A) is followed by a swing high (Point B), and then followed by a breakdown of this swing low (Point A), a short sale can be executed. A short position at this breakdown may have only an even chance of being profitable but moves that turn out to be profitable will be huge gainers. However, the trader may also have to accept the few small losses before getting a large move on the downside. In the case of a contra-trend trade, it is advisable to put up only half the risk capital (1% of the capital) as compared to the pro-trend signal.

Reversal Trade

The reversal signal may also be of two types.

One situation is where the contra-trend sell signal fails immediately — i.e. before the 8DMA line has a chance of going below the 21DMA line — and hits the stop loss. In this case, the short position should be exited and a long position simultaneously be created at the same level, but with only half the risk (1% of capital) since the market is quite overbought already and may start correcting any time.

The other situation is where the 8DMA line falls below the 21DMA line after the sell signal. In this case, a renewed buy trade is to be taken in the same manner as our pro-trend buy signal with full risk (2% of the capital) since the 13WMA line is still above the 34WMA line and this buy signal is occurring after a proper correction.

Entries and Exits

As per our system criteria, a buy trade is initiated when a swing high is broken on the upside — and a sell signal is initiated when a swing low is broken on the downside.

Figure 16.1 is the daily chart of Nifty futures. The trend indicated by the weekly chart was up since the 13WMA line was above the 34WMA line during this period (not shown in Figure 16.1). Once the 8DMA line goes below the 21DMA line, the trader should be prepared to buy on a swing breakout, which in this case happened on 26 February when the prices broke out above the previous swing high of 4,928 established on 17 February. The entry in such a trade should be made by putting a buy stop loss just above the level of 4,928, say, at 4,938.

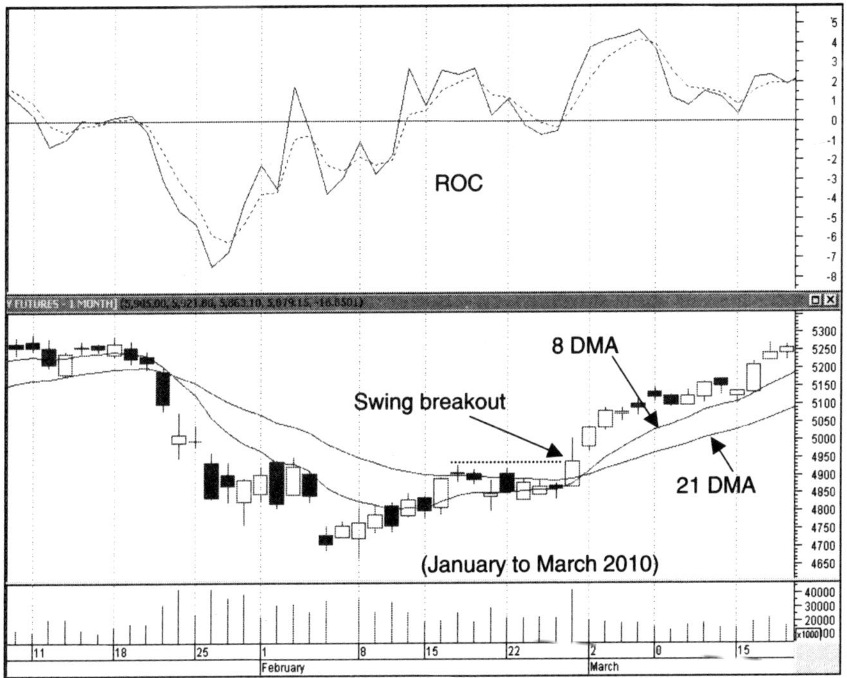

Figure 16.1: **Daily chart** of **Nifty futures. The horizontal dotted line indicates the level of the swing breakout**

~

There are two ways to make an entry into a long position. One would have been to wait for Nifty to cross the level of 4,928 and then execute the buy trade. Another way is to put a buy stop loss above the level of 4,928 and wait for the trade to get executed. The latter is the preferred entry method since it almost guarantees that our long position will get established.

Once the trade is entered, an initial stop loss is to be entered below the level of 4,797, the swing low created on 19 February. The actual stop loss would be 4,787. The trade should be carried forward till the time the swing low is not broken. In this case, the initial stop loss remained intact till the right edge of the chart in Figure 16.1.

Short positions are created by using a sell stop loss in a similar manner, namely by placing the initial stop loss above the corresponding swing high once the trade is entered. Stop loss can be trailed downward if the price falls and lower swing highs are created. The trade is ultimately exited if either the initial or the trailing stop loss, whatever the case may be, is hit.

As can be seen from the chart in Figure 16.2, a new swing low was formed on 19 April 2010 at a level of 5,162, followed by another swing high on 26 April. The swing low of 19 April was broken on 4 May and the long position initiated at the level of 4,938 was exited at the trailing stop loss of 5,152, generating a

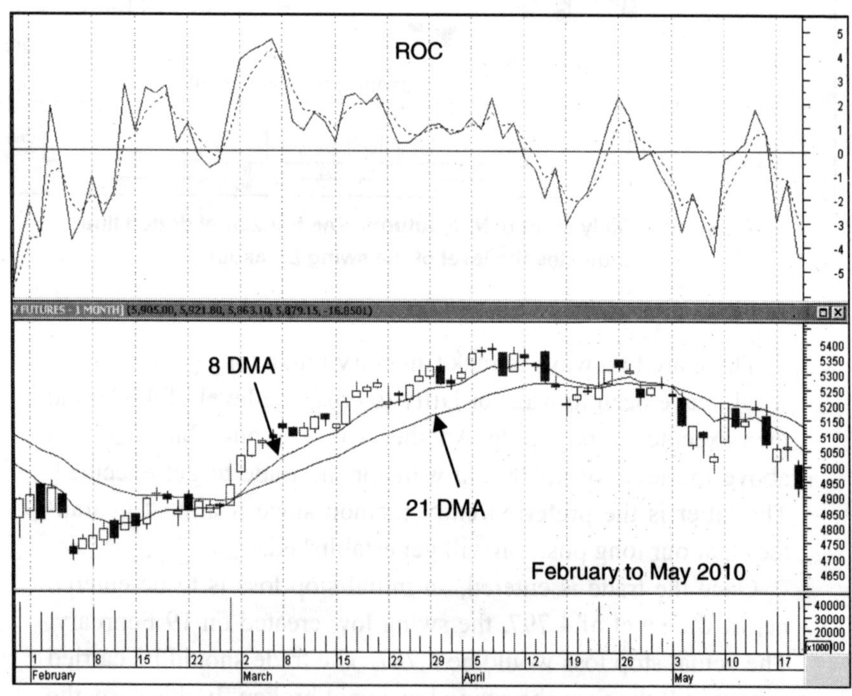

Figure 16.2: **Daily chart of Nifty futures**

handsome profit of 214 points (4.3%) in this trade. This profit of 4.3% is without taking into account that the position was created by using margin of approximately 15%, so the actual profit on capital deployed was 29%.

Position Size

There is no doubt that the percentage risk method (equal risk) of position sizing works best with the trading system described in this book. Let us assume that a per trade risk of ₹50,000 is being taken. The position size is then to be calculated as below:

$$\text{Position Size (number of shares)} = \frac{50{,}000}{(\text{Entry price} - \text{Initial stop loss})}$$

In the example in Figure 16.2:

$$\text{Position Size} = \frac{50{,}000}{4{,}938 - 4{,}787} = \frac{50{,}000}{151} = 331$$

Since one contract of Nifty was of 50 shares at the time this trade was taken, the trader would have bought 7 lots of Nifty future contracts to make a total of 350 shares. (From 2017, one contract of Nifty futures comprises of 75 shares, so one would have needed to buy 4 lots and the calculation can be modified accordingly).

Since the trade was exited at the level of ₹5,152, the profit per share on this trade was:

Profit per share = ₹5,152 – 4,938 = ₹214

Total profit = 214 × 350 (number of shares) = ₹74,900.

The total value of Nifty future contracts purchased in the above example was ₹17,28,300 (350 shares @ ₹4,938 each). However, since futures contracts are typically bought and sold on margin of 10% to 15% of the contract value, the trader is required to deposit a maximum of 15% of ₹17,28,300 which is ₹2,59,245. With a deposit of only ₹2,59,245, the trader would have been able to earn ₹74,900 (minus the brokerage) which works out to a profit of approximately 29%. The brokerage in this trade would not be more than a thousand rupees. The maximum risk in the trade was only ₹50,000. There was no danger of the risk getting out of control except in the rare chance of a gap opening in the market.

~

17

~

Real-Life Trading Using the Daily Chart

It is one thing to make a profitable trading system and an entirely different thing to actually implement it in real life. Back in the days when I was new to trading, and often found it rather difficult to stick to the discipline it required, I wrote:

Trade is to be entered
Risk is to be calculated
Stop loss is to be activated
Profit is to be captivated.

It is necessary for the reader to go through the examples that follow slowly, without haste, in order to fully grasp the nuances of this trading system. It has been explained earlier that initially it is not easy to "make a killing" through trading but as your knowledge and experience grow, you should discover that the process of making money has become "automatic, mechanical and, boring" for you.

The real-life trading examples in the chapter are based only on Nifty trades. This helps remove the selection bias, for it is easy to show selected examples from different individual stocks where stupendous gains were made. Being an average of large cap stocks, Nifty behaves in a more balanced manner. Furthermore, no mechanical system can be "proved" by picking up random trades from here and there. Therefore, a reasonably long period must be selected and continuous trading has to be shown for the system to carry any value. The system being propounded in this book tries to filter out trades occurring in sideways markets and picks out only those situations when most of the factors are aligned together in the same direction.

Our examples of real life trades are based on the daily charts of Nifty futures during the period from 1 January to 31 December 2010.

During this entire period, the 13-week EMA line was above the 34-week EMA line and hence, the long term trend as indicated by the weekly chart was up (*see* Figure 17.1).

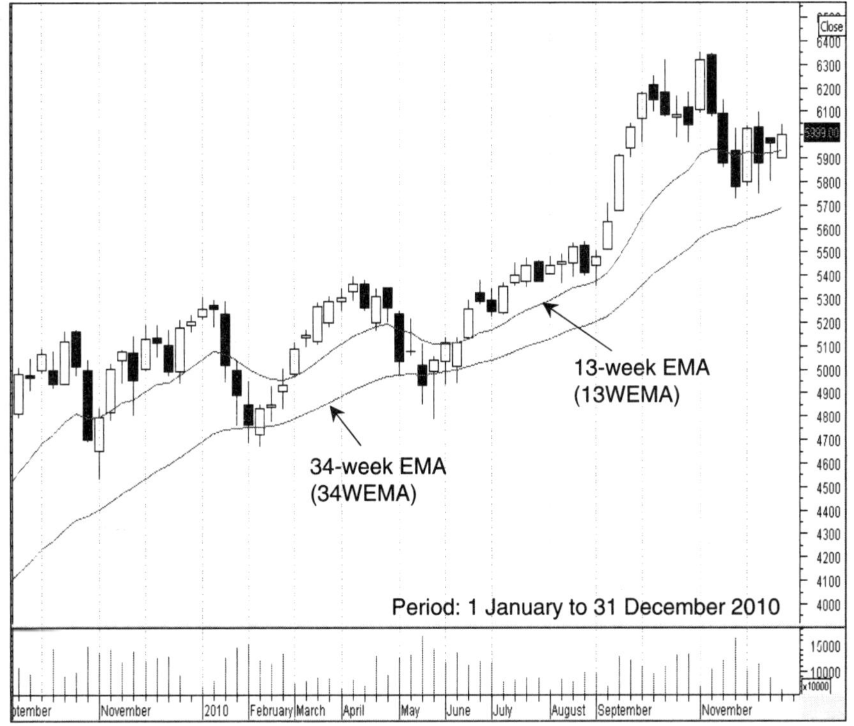

Figure 17.1: **Weekly chart of Nifty futures shows an uptrend in force with the 13-week EMA line above the 34-week EMA line throughout the period covered in the chart**

~

Trade-1

The first signal as per our trading system was generated on 26 February when Nifty crossed the swing high of 4,928 established earlier on 17 February. A stop loss was placed at the swing low of 4,797 established on 19 February. The position size was calculated on the basis of a fixed amount of risk of ₹50,000 per trade as follows:

$$\text{Position size} = \frac{50{,}000}{\text{Entry price} - \text{Stop loss}} = \frac{50{,}000}{4928 - 4797} = 382$$

Thus, 382 units of Nifty futures were to be purchased but as the lot size of Nifty futures was at that time fixed at 50 — and also to account for the difference in the estimated stop loss and actual stop loss — 7 lots of Nifty futures equivalent to 350 units of Nifty futures were bought at a price of 4,928 each. In practice, however, the entry price would have been approximately 4,938 as the trade would have to be entered by putting a buy stop loss above the level of 4,928 and a leeway of 0.2% should be allowed when entering trades based on daily time frame. As already explained, the estimated initial stop loss is the price shown at the low of the ROC swing in the chart whereas the actual stop loss is slightly below so that the stop loss is not hit by market noise. In the example given above, the estimated initial stop loss as shown by the chart is at 4,797 whereas the actual initial stop loss would have been 4,787. We can then re-calculate our position size as below:

$$\frac{50{,}000}{\text{Entry price} - \text{Stop loss}} = \frac{50{,}000}{4938 - 4787} = 331$$

Since the standard risk amount per trade has been fixed as ₹50,000, the full amount was risked in this trade as per the trading system. This was a pro-trend buy signal occurring after a full correction in the daily chart, as the 8DMA line had gone below the 21DMA line on 25 January.

The trade progressed satisfactorily till 19 April when another swing low was created by our ROC based mechanical swing — the second panel from the top in Figure 17.2 — with the Nifty level at 5,162. This low was followed by another swing high and the low of 5,162 was broken subsequently on 4 May, at which time the long position was exited. The actual exit price would have been 5,152.

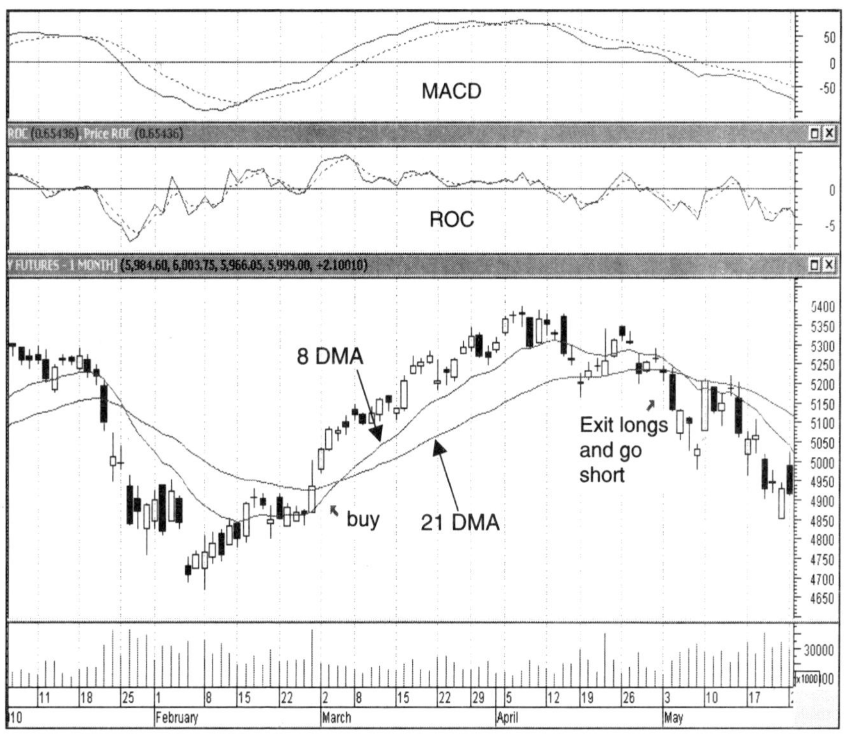

Figure 17.2: **Daily chart of Nifty futures highlighting the various aspects of Trade-1**

~

The profit made in this trade, without taking into account any slippage (due to difference in estimated entry and exit prices and the prices at which the entry and exit was actually made) and brokerage was ₹82,040 as follows:

Profit = (Exit price – Entry price) × Position size
= (5,162 – 4,928) ×350 = ₹82,040

The capital employed in the trade would have been:

(Purchase price x position size) x (15÷100)
= (4928 x 350) x (15/100)
= ₹2,58,720

Trade-2

On 13 April, the solid line of daily MACD crossed the dotted line to the downside and the MACD thus went into sell mode, as you can see in the uppermost panel in Figure 17.3. The trading system under consideration requires that a new swing low needs to be created, either simultaneously or after — but not before — the MACD goes into sell mode for us to contemplate a short position. In this case, a swing low was duly created on 19 April at the level of 5,162. Thereafter, as per our system, a new swing high was needed to be created, which occurred on 26 April with Nifty at 5,347. The trader should now be trying to establish a short position if and when Nifty breaks the low of 5,162 with a stop loss at the level of 5,347. Because the longer term trend as per the weekly chart was still up, the risk to be taken on the short position should be half of the usual risk, i.e. ₹25,000 (half of ₹50,000).

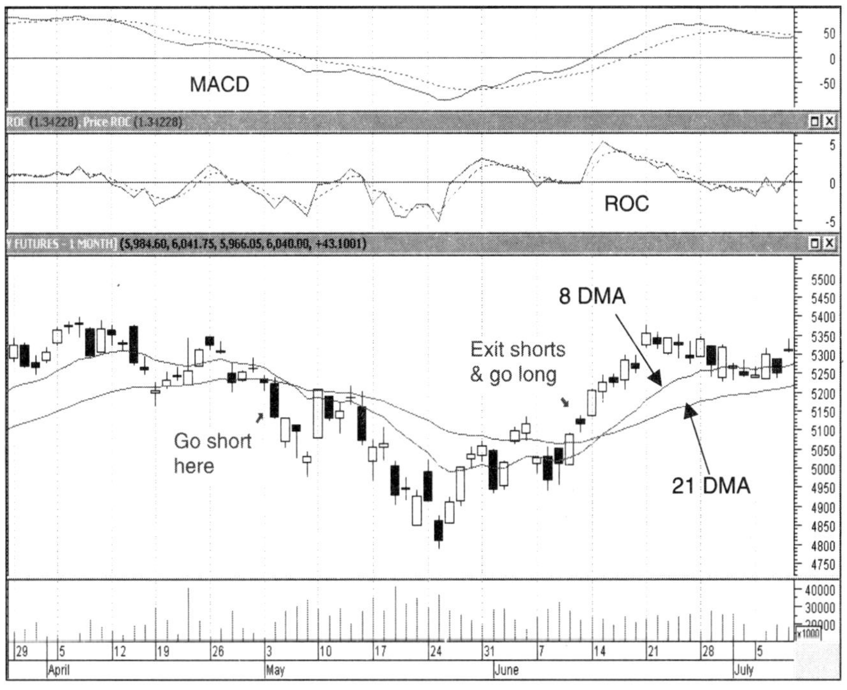

Figure 17.3: **Daily chart of Nifty showing Trade-2 with entry and exit points of the counter-trend short trade highlighted**

~

The position size for Trade-2 would be calculated as under:

$$\text{Position size} = \frac{25{,}000}{\text{Stop loss} - \text{Entry price}}$$

$$= \frac{25{,}000}{5{,}347 - 5{,}162} = 135$$

Thus, the trader should have sold 2 or 3 lots of Nifty futures at this point.

Thereafter, Nifty then kept falling and created another swing low at 4,976, followed by a swing high at 5,218 on 13 May, followed by still another swing low at 4,786 on 25 May. Once the swing low of 25 May was created, the stop loss could have been shifted from 5,347 to 5,218. This was followed by another swing high with Nifty at 5,135 on 4 June, and then another swing low on 8 June at 4,937. The stop loss would then get shifted to 5,135 and this was hit on 11 June when the short position would have been exited.

The profit in this trade was ₹2,740.

Trade-3

Since the long term trend was still up according to the weekly chart, exiting the short position of Trade-2 would have also offered the opportunity for a simultaneous long trade. As the 8DMA line had gone below the 21DMA line during this period, a long position with the full amount of risk (₹50,000) would have been established on 11 June at the Nifty level of 5,135, with a stop loss below the level of 4,937 which was the swing low established on 8 June (*see* Figure 17.4). The trader would have bought 253 units of Nifty, equivalent to 5 lots of 50 each.

The next swing low was created on 30 June with Nifty at 5,225, which was followed by a swing high of 5,454 on 14 July. The stop loss would now be shifted to the low of 5,225. A further swing low on 20 July with Nifty at 5,350 was followed by a swing high on 23 July. The trailing stop loss would now be placed below 5,350. Still another swing low occurred at 5,369 on 30 July, followed by a swing high on 9 August with Nifty at 5,489. The trailing stop loss would now get shifted to below 5,369, the most recent swing low.

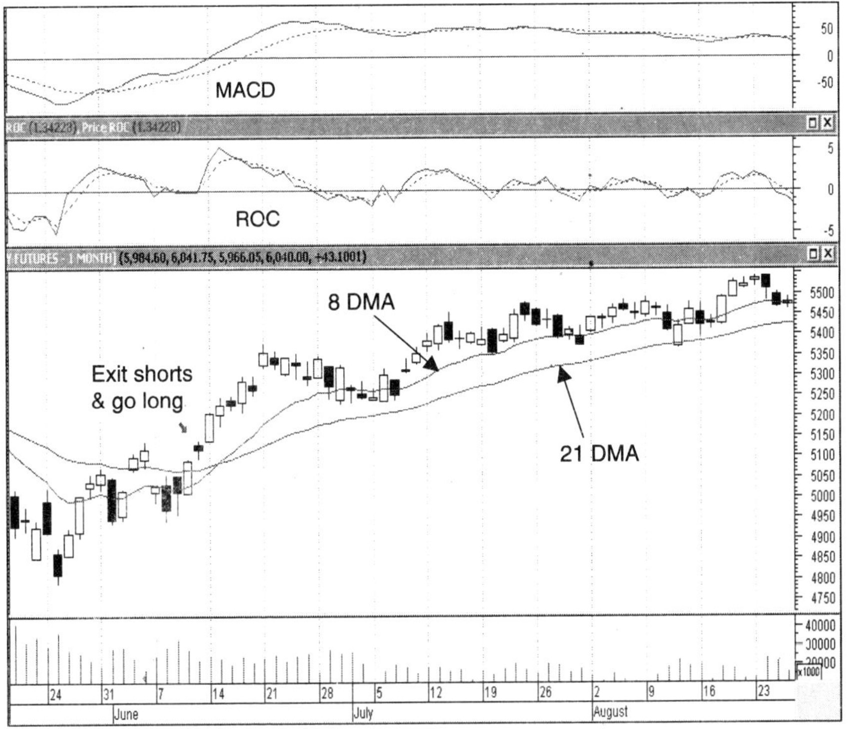

Figure 17.4: **Daily chart of Nifty showing the entry point for the long Trade-3**

~

Another swing low was, thereafter, created at 5,364 on 12 August. This was below the level of the previously decided stop loss of 5,369. However, as described in Chapter 9, the actual stop loss should be different from the estimated stop loss level. Since the recommended difference between the two for trading the daily charts is 0.2% of the Nifty level, the actual stop loss would have been placed at 5,359 and not at 5,369. And this level did not get hit during this chart's duration.

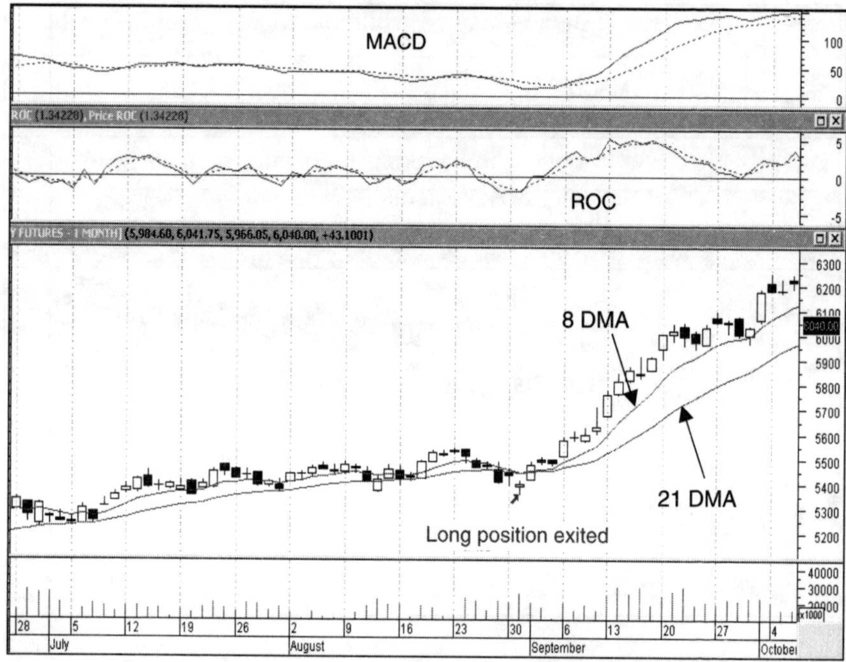

Figure 17.5: **Daily chart showing the Trade-3 exit when the trailing stop loss was hit**

~

Another swing high was then created on 23 August at 5,543. The trailing stop loss at 5,359 was subsequently hit when the price created a low of 5,356 on 31 August (*see* Figure 17.5).

The profit in this trade was ₹58,550, with the full risk of ₹50,000.

Although the price broke the previous swing low, there was no occasion to go short here. Remember, for a contra-trend short position to be taken, it is necessary that the following sequence of events takes place:

- The daily MACD must go into sell mode;
- A swing low must be created thereafter or simultaneously — but not before the MACD goes into sell mode;

- Another swing high is created while the MACD is still in sell mode;
- This is followed by the break of the previous swing low.

Readers would note while making the swing high of 23 August at 5,543, the daily MACD actually went into buy mode.

Trade-4

Since the longer trend as shown by the weekly chart was still up at the end of Trade-3 and the 8DMA line had gone below the

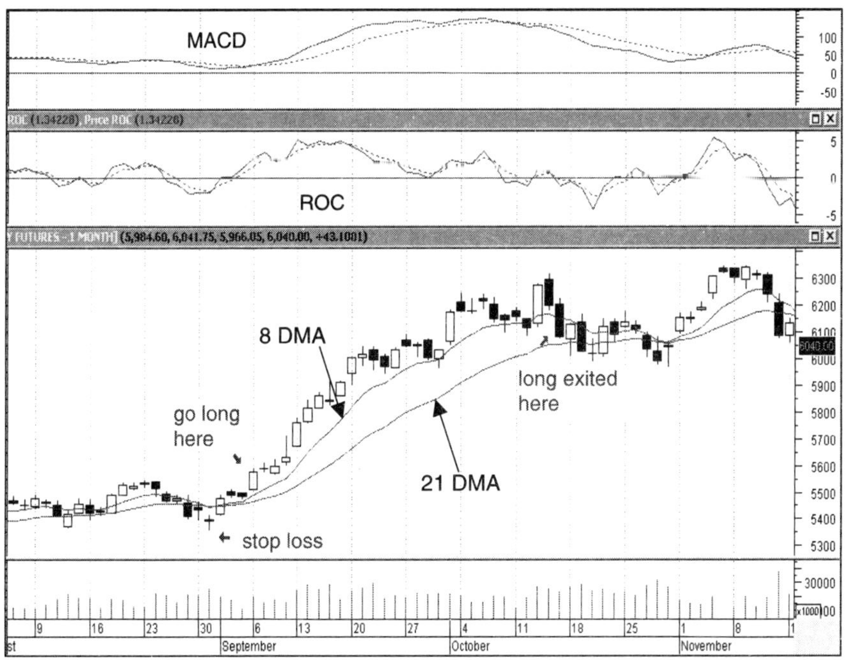

Figure 17.6: **Trade-4 depicted on Nifty's daily chart, with entry, stop loss and exit highlighted**

~

21DMA line on 31 August — albeit for only one day but this should not be of any concern because we are following a mechanical strategy here — the trader would have again gone long on the break of the swing high of 5,543 created on 23 August. Entry was made on 6 September with a stop loss below the swing low of 5,356 (*see* Figure 17.6).

The position size was calculated to be 5 lots. The trade was exited on 15 October at the level of 6,083 when the price broke the swing low of 6,083 created on 12 October. While the uptrend was in progress, the initial stop loss would have gradually trailed up to the level of 6,083.

The profit in this trade was ₹1,35,025, based on the full risk amount of ₹50,000.

Trade-5

On 8 October 2010, the daily MACD went into sell mode, simultaneously making a swing low of 6,083, followed by the swing high of 6,318. The MACD was still in sell mode when the swing low of 6,083 was broken on 15 October. Not only should the trader have exited his long position here, as we did in the case of Trade-4, he should also immediately have gone short with a stop loss above the high of 6,318 with half the usual amount of risk.

Why half the risk? Because the long term trend in the weekly chart was still up and this is thus a counter-trend trade. Only 2 lots of Nifty would have to be sold by risking 1% of capital. As you can see in Figure 17.7, the trade was subsequently exited on 3 November when the price broke the swing high of 6,180 established on 25 October.

The net loss on this trade was ₹9,700, having taken a risk of ₹25,000.

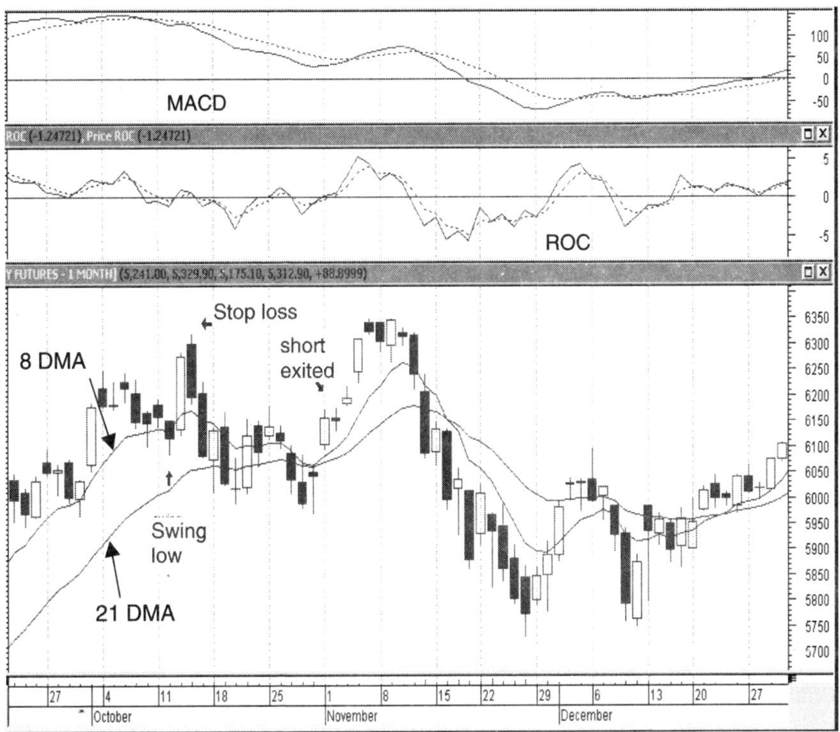

Figure 17.7: **Daily chart showing the countertrend Trade-5, with the entry, stop loss and exit of this short trade**

~

Trade-6

Since Nifty's longer trend as per weekly chart was still up at the closure of Trade-5, the trader would now go long above the level of 6,180, the swing high created on 25 October 2010. Only half the usual amount of risk would have been taken as the 8DMA line did not go below the 21DMA line, resulting in the buying of two lots of Nifty. The stop loss on this trade was placed below

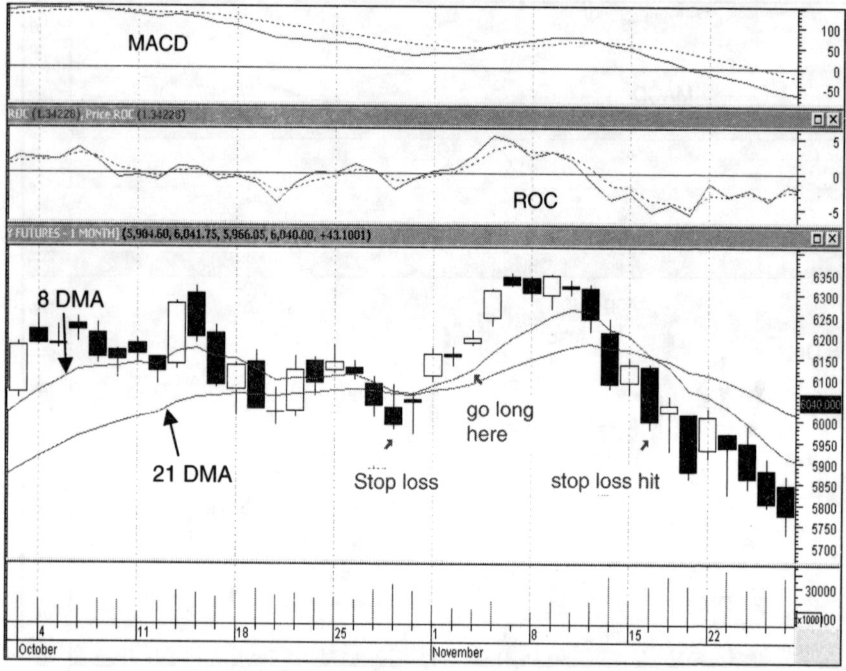

Figure 17.8: **Daily chart of Nifty showing Trade-6, a long trade that resulted in a total loss of the capital at risk**

~

the 29 October swing low of 5,966, which was subsequently broken (*see* Figure 17.8). Since there was no occasion to raise the stop loss in this trade, the total amount at risk was lost.

Loss = Buy price 6,180 – Exit price 5,966 = 214

Loss per share = 6,180 – 5,966 = 214

Total loss on 2 lots of Nifty = 100 x 214 = 21,400

Hence, the loss in this trade was ₹21,400.

~

No other signal was generated as per our system till the end of 2010 (*see* Figure 17.9).

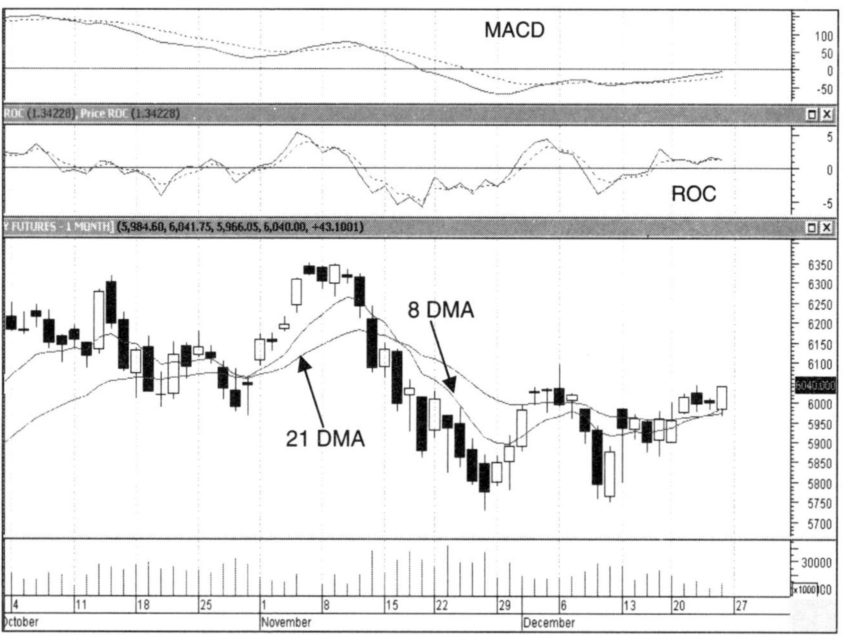

Figure 17.9: **Daily chart of Nifty, from October to December 2010, during which our system did not generate any further signals**

~

Net Profit for the Year

The cumulative profit for all the trades during the year was as follows:

Trade	(₹)
Trade-1	+ 82,040
Trade-2	+ 2,740
Trade-3	+ 58,550
Trade-4	+1,35,025
Trade-5	- 9,700
Trade-6	- 21,400
Total of Trades	**+2,47,255**

(*Note:* The actual profits would have been a little lower due to slippage and brokerage, etc.)

The maximum amount of margin money which was required during the period was not more than ₹2,50,000 at any stage. The maximum number of lots (7) were bought in Trade-1 which amounted to buying a total of 350 units of Nifty at the price of 4,928, with a total value of ₹17,24,800.

Assuming the margin to be 15%, the capital required for carrying out this trade would have been only ₹2,58,720.

Even if the trader had kept an amount of ₹2,50,000 as surplus funds to take care of losing trades, his total capital outlay would have been approximately ₹5,00,000. Thus he was able to generate approximately 50 % return during this period of one year.

Incidentally, most brokers accept fixed deposit receipts of banks instead of cash margin and hence your total capital also earns interest, in addition to the profits mentioned above. The risk of ₹50,000 mentioned here is to be taken on each trade if the trader has a capital of ₹25 lakh. This will allow him five trades at any one time, each requiring ₹5 lakh for meeting margin money and drawdown requirements.

Caveat

It must be highlighted that there is no guarantee that the system will generate similar profits every year. This is particularly true when trading on the basis of daily charts because only 5 to 10 trades are generated every year which cannot be depended upon statistically to give a regular income. That is why trading on the basis of daily chart is more useful for those having some other regular source of income as well. Traders who are looking for regular income from trading itself, will find it more suitable to trade in 15-minute charts which will generate a larger number of trades resulting in a more regular income but this will require them to be present at the trading terminal throughout the market hours. Alternatively, the trader may choose to track 8 to 10 different stocks and trade their signals on daily charts. This would enable the trader to generate profit on a yearly basis. Care should be taken to choose stocks from different sectors of the economy.

How the Fearless Trading System Performed During the Market Fall of 2018

Some readers would be wondering whether I may have chosen a period which is conducive to the success of my trading system. This is really not the case. I had completed the book's draft at the

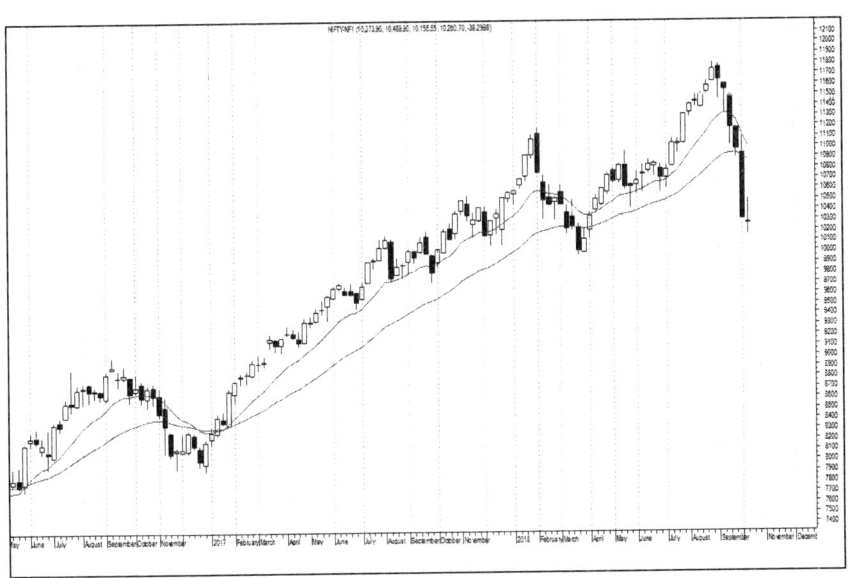

Figure 17.10: **Weekly chart of Nifty showing that the trend had turned upward on 27 January 2017**

~

end of year 2010 and had taken the most recent example of that time. My learned publisher now wants me to show the readers as to how my system would have performed in the market crash of 2018.

Nifty futures made a high of 11,793 on 31 August 2018 and started falling thereafter, reaching 10,294 on 5 October 2018, which was a fall of approximately 13% in about a one-month period.

Even during this period, our system performed exceedingly well. Figure 17.10 shows that the 13WMA went above 34WMA on 27 January 2017 and has not gone down since till the time of this writing. The most recent trade on the daily chart was generated on 9 July 2018 when Nifty crossed its previous swing high

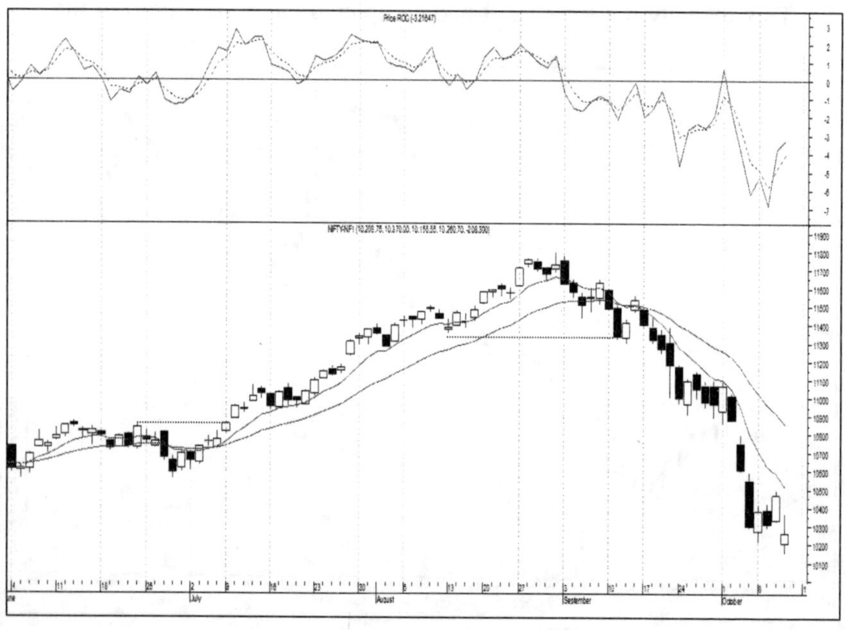

Figure 17.11: **Daily chart of Nifty showing the long trade executed during July to September 2018**

of 10,849 as shown by Figure 17.11. The stop loss in this trade was at 10,557. Nifty rose thereafter providing a trailing stop loss of 11,354 which was taken out on 11 September 2018 and so the trade was exited. The profit in this trade was 505 points (4.6% without the use of margin). Not only was the trade exited at a handsome profit but even the subsequent market fall failed to hurt the trader. However, as per our system the trader was unable to establish a short position to take advantage of this fall.

~

18

Short Term Trading

One of the major advantages of technical analysis over fundamental analysis is that the former can be applied to all time frames. Although most traders are comfortable trading in daily charts, those who are watching the markets throughout the day can also make extra profits in shorter term trading. It could either be intra-day trading where trades are squared before the market close, or trades spanning approximately 1 to 3 days.

- For intra-day trading, the trader would need to trade on the basis of 5-minute charts.
- For trades lasting 1 to 3 days, 15-minute charts are more suitable.

The system for short term trading need not be complex. For example, a trader desiring to trade the 15-minute chart should first determine the direction of the trend on the daily chart, and then take a short term position in the direction of the daily trend.

As a general rule, it is not advisable to take contra-trend trades in such short time frame trades.

To determine the trend in the daily chart, all that we need is to check whether 13DMA is above (uptrend) or below 34 DMA (downtrend).

Let's consider an example.

On 11 January 2011, the 13-day moving average of Nifty futures crossed below the 34-day moving average line, marking the beginning of a downtrend.

The trader would now look for an upward correction in Nifty's 15-minute chart which would be confirmed once the 8-period MA, plotted on the 15-minute price chart, goes above the 21-period MA plotted on the 15-minute price chart. Once this happens, a short position can be initiated on the break of a mechanical swing.

It needs to be emphasized that the 8-period MA is not an average of the price of 8 minutes but is an average of 8 periods of 15 minutes each; and so is the case with 21-period MA.

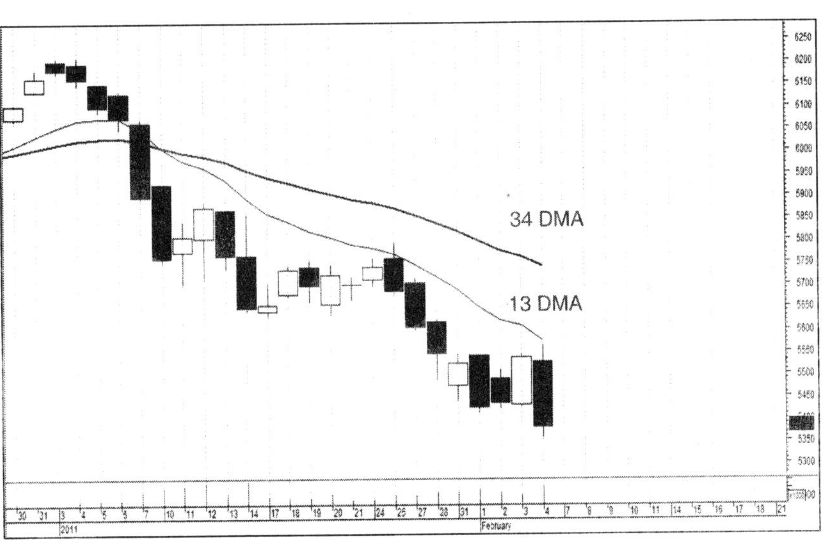

Figure 18.1: **The trend of Nifty futures in the daily chart had turned downward on 11 January 2011 when the 13DMA line went below the 34DMA line**

~

Trade-1

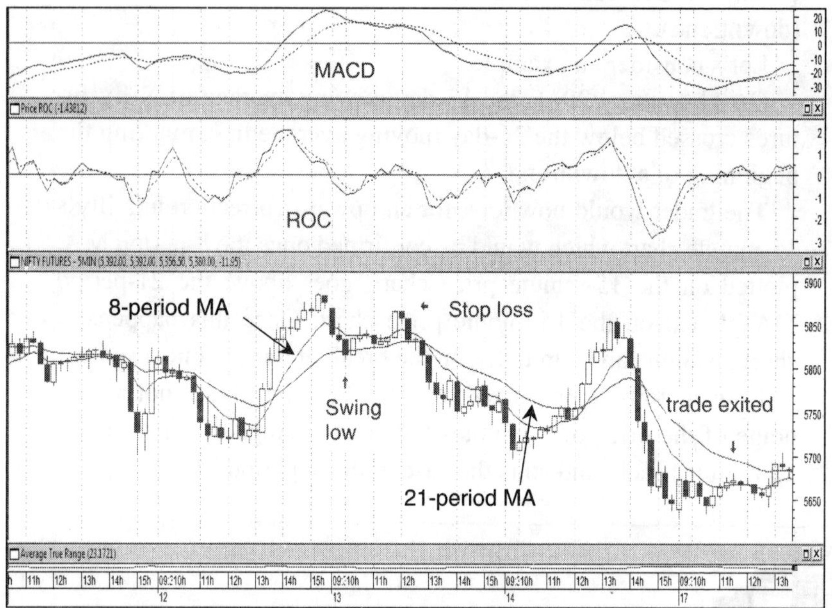

Figure 18.2: **Trade-1 parameters shown on Nifty's 15-minute chart**

~

Figure 18.2 highlights that the trader could have gone short when the swing low of 5,810, established at 10A.M. on 13 January was broken on the downside. The stop loss on this trade would have been placed at the swing high of 5,867.

In such a short term trade, it's not advisable to take more than one-fourth the risk of the daily chart since there may be numerous whipsaws in a 15-minute chart. So, a trader assuming a risk of ₹50,000 on daily chart trades should not take a risk higher than ₹12,500 on a 15-minute chart trade. Overall, 219 units of Nifty futures would have been shorted (4 lots equaling 200 Nifty). The trade was exited at the level of 5,681.

Profit = Sell price – Buy price
= 5,810 – 5,681 = 129
Total Profit = 129 x 200 = ₹25,800

Thus, the profit in this trade was ₹25,800.

Trade-2

As you would see in Figure 18.3, the 8-period MA line in the 15-minute chart once again crossed the 21-period MA line on the upside. The short position was taken when the swing low of 5,721 was broken. This low had been established at 10 A.M. on 19 January. The stop loss was placed at the swing high of 5,754.

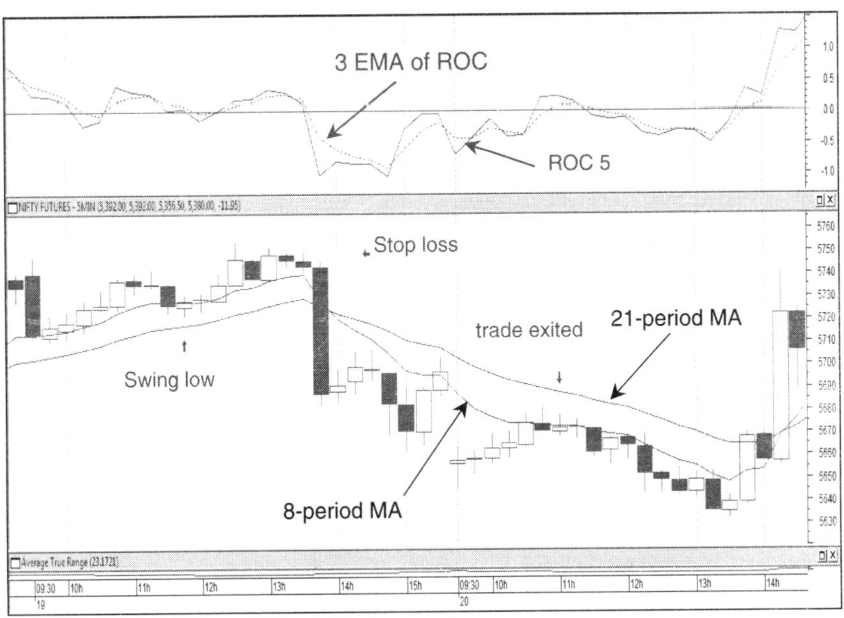

Figure 18.3: **15-minute chart of Nifty futures showing Trade-2**

~

The trade was exited on 29 January at the level of 5,681. 7 lots of Nifty were shorted for a total risk of ₹12,500.

Profit = Sell price– Buy price
=5,721 – 5,681 = 40
Total Profit = 40 x 350 = ₹14,000

The profit in this trade was ₹14,000.

Trade-3

As you can see in Figure 18.4, a short position was entered when the swing low of 5,692 established at 1P.M. on 21 January was broken. The stop loss was placed at the level of 5,717 and,

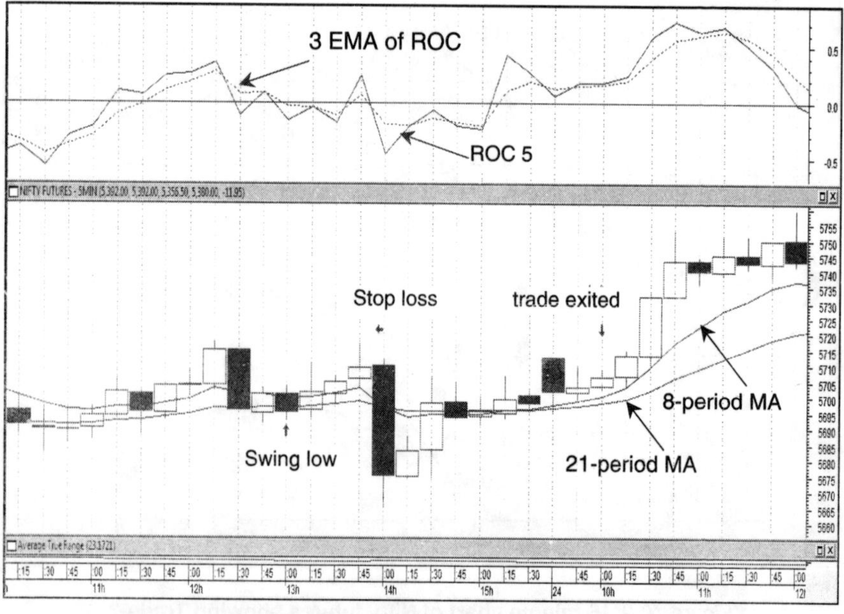

Figure 18.4: **15-minute chart of Nifty futures detailing Trade-3**

~

as it turned out, the trade was exited at the initial stop loss level itself at a loss.

The risk per unit of Nifty was 25 points (5,717-5,692). The risk amount of ₹12,500, divided by 25, permitted us to sell 500 units. Since each lot consisted of 50 units, 10 lots were shorted. As the stop loss of 5,717 was hit, the total amount at risk was lost. Hence the loss in this trade was ₹12,500.

Loss = Sell price – Buy price
= 5,717 – 5,692 = 25
Total Profit =-25 X 500 = ₹-12,500

Trade-4

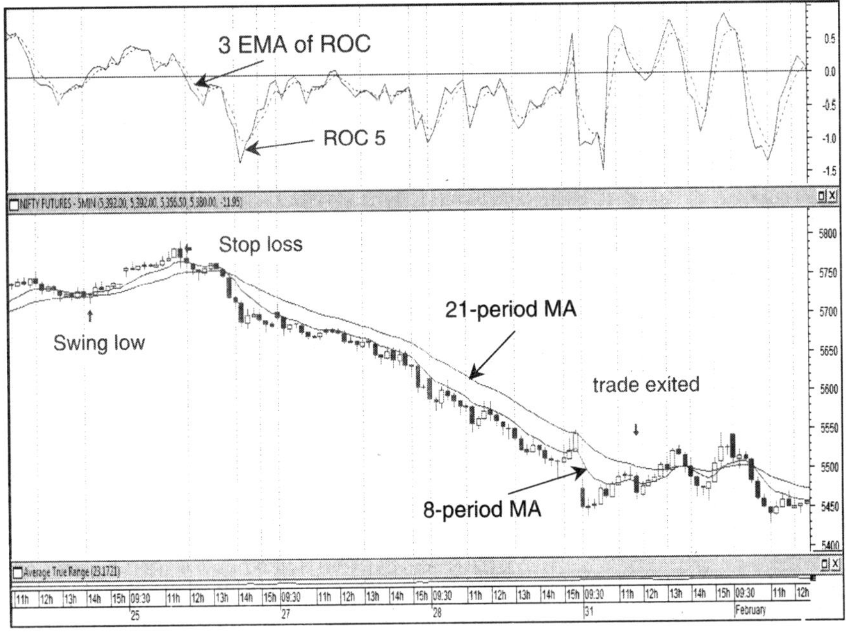

Figure 18.5: **Trade-4 highlighted on the 15-minute chart of Nifty futures**

~

An upward correction resulted in a new short position below the swing low of 5,716 being established at 11.45 A.M. on 25 January. The stop loss was placed at 5,796. The trade was subsequently exited at 5,501 on 31 January. Again, as this was a pro-trend trade, full risk of ₹12,500 was taken. 3 lots of Nifty were shorted as we were permitted to short 156 units only.

The total profit made in this trade was ₹32,250.

~

Total Profit

The total profit in the four trades was ₹59,550 over a period of 18 days. The actual profits would have been slightly lower due to slippage and brokerage costs.

Although the system highlighted above requires the trader to analyze the market during market hours, this should not be considered an intraday system because the positions are not closed by the end of the day. The position can be carried over to next day and closed only when the trailing stop loss is hit.

~

19

~

Time Diversification

It is advantageous to trade in two or more time frames if the trader has the requisite time and capital. For example, it will be seen that while the system may not sometimes generate a buy signal on a daily chart, even though the price may advance quite significantly thereafter, a profitable buy signal may well be generated on the hourly chart during that period. Equally, it must be pointed out that no system is perfect and every system will leave out some profitable trades.

One of the systems that can keep the trader in all types of markets, whether uptrending, downtrending or sideways, is based on moving average crossovers. For example, if the 8-day moving average goes above the 21-day moving average, then a long position is established while if the averages cross in the opposite direction, the long position is exited and a short position is also established simultaneously. These systems are highly specific and objective but suffer from two defects which are well known — and yet worth repeating:

1. Moving average signals occur quite late.

2. Such systems do not work well in sideways markets. The drawdowns when using such a system are sometimes huge and few traders have the mental strength of continuing with the system after that.

Another benefit of trading in multiple time frames is that unless the price has already moved considerably — say by about 5% in case of the index and by approximately 10% in individual stocks — a buy signal may not be generated in the daily chart. For those watching the markets throughout the day, making an entry at such a late stage can be very uncomfortable whereas by using multiple time frames, a trader can build up his long positions at much lower levels.

Furthermore, just before the final exit, prices may fall quite significantly before the trailing stop loss is hit and it is natural at these times to feel disappointed that paper profits have gotten eroded. Although there is no guarantee about this, but it's possible that a sell trade signal as per the system received on hourly or 15-minute charts may let the trader build a short position at a higher level. This will keep the trader stay more or less neutral in the market, since he would be long on the basis of the daily chart and short on the basis of the lower time frame chart. Any further fall in the price at this juncture would not disturb him emotionally since erosion to his capital has been prevented. It is necessary to point out that accomplishing this may require taking a few contra-trend signals on smaller time frame charts. However, these will be more in the nature of either profit booking or going neutral rather than creating naked positions.

Another way of using a combination of multiple time frames has also been suggested. Let's suppose the trader is trying to establish a long position as per the daily chart and the formation of the set up for making a long entry (a pro-trend buy signal) is complete. While using the system propounded in this book, at

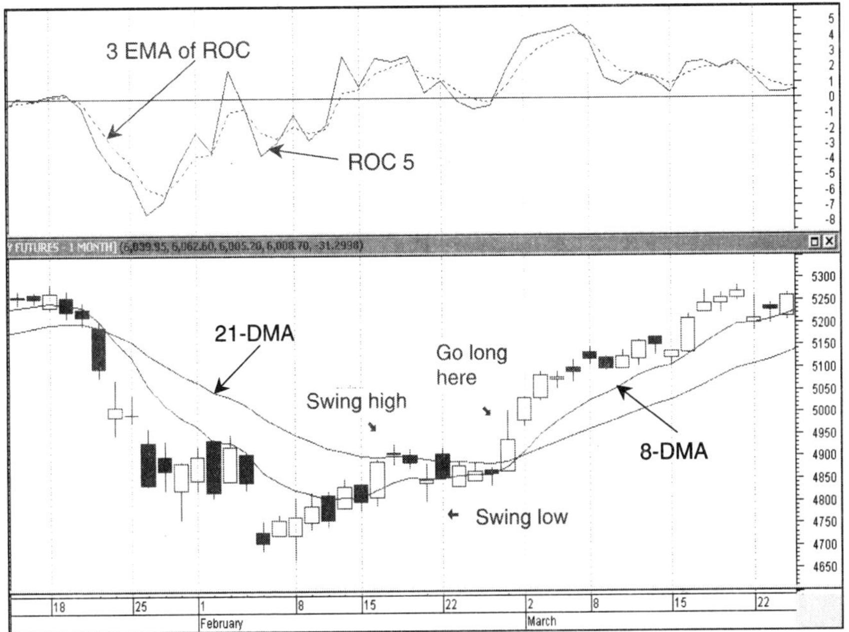

Figure 19.1: **Daily chart of Nifty futures**

~

such a juncture, the trend as per the weekly chart would be up and the 8DMA line would have gone below the 21 DMA line.

Let us consider an example.

On 24 February 2010, the ROC based mechanical swing had gone below the zero line in the chart in Figure 19.1. The longer term trend indicated by the weekly chart was up at this time (though not shown here), and a trader using the daily chart would have tried to establish a long position only when the price broke out of the previous swing high of 4,928 created on 17 February. The stop loss in this trade would have been below 4,797, which was the swing low of 19 February. The trade entry would have been made on 26 February. For a risk amount of ₹50,000, approximately 381 units of Nifty futures would have been purchased.

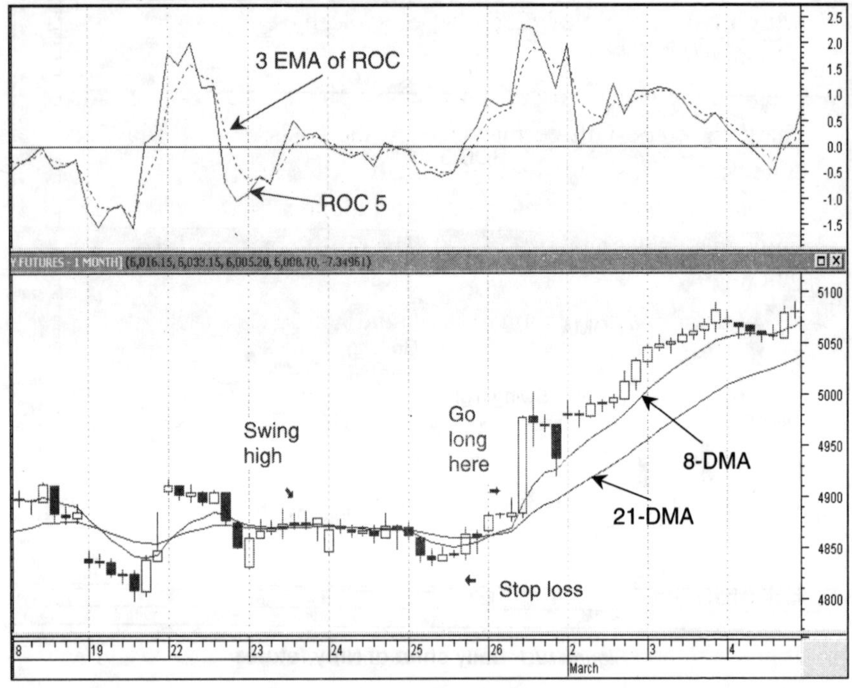

Figure 19.2: **Hourly chart of Nifty futures**

~

On the other hand, a trader combining multiple time frames would have started to look at Nifty's hourly chart once it was evident that the ROC based mechanical swing had gone below the zero line on the daily chart, which happened on 24 February (*see* Figure 19.1).

Once the ROC based mechanical swing went below the zero line in the daily chart, the trader would have attempted to establish a long position upon the breakout of any ROC based swing high on the hourly chart. The swing high at 4,889 on 23 February was followed by a swing low of 4,832 on 25 February 2010 (*see* Figure 19.2). A long position would be established on the break of 4,889 with a stop loss of 4,832. The trader would have been able to establish his long position at 4,889 instead of 4,928. Even with a risk amount of ₹25,000, he would have been able to buy 440 units of Nifty.

Once the price crosses the swing high of 4,928 on the daily chart, the trade will be managed on the basis of only the daily time frame. This trade was thus finally exited at 5,162.

The profit by using the daily chart alone was ₹89,154 on 381 units on a risk capital of ₹50,000. The profit per unit of Nifty was 234 points.

By using a combination of daily and hourly charts the profit is ₹1,20,120 on 440 units on a risk capital of ₹25,000. The profit per unit of Nifty was 273 points in this case.

In this manner, the trader was not only able to reduce his initial risk but was also able to buy more units of Nifty and increase his profit substantially.

Caution

It needs to be emphasized that considerable experience would be required before one is able to use multiple time frames advantageously. There would also be occasions when an early entry on the basis of an hourly chart may not be carried over to daily chart and the trader may have to book an unnecessary loss. That is why it may be better to buy only half the total quantity on a signal based on the hourly chart and the balance should be bought once the signal is confirmed on the daily chart.

> Lower risk should be taken in smaller time frames — the risk should be 50% for trades based on hourly charts, and 25% in the case of trades on 15-minute charts as compared to the risk in the case of trades on daily charts.

~

20

~

How to Hedge Your Portfolio with Nifty Futures

Even traders have investment portfolios. And unlike most investors who are hardly bothered about the day to day market fluctuations, traders using a sound method of technical analysis would prefer to take some concrete action when their analysis points to a downfall in the market. This can be done by hedging the long term portfolio either by short selling Nifty futures or by buying put options.

One of the problems investment portfolios face is the lack of an exit strategy. Whereas a trader first decides his stop loss level and then enters a trade, this is not often the case with an investment portfolio. Neither may it be desirable to dissolve and create portfolios frequently. The falling value of a portfolio is creates fear in the investor's mind. Accordingly, good assets may well be dumped at a time which may actually be the best opportunity to be buying. Whatever the reason, few investors are able to protect their investment portfolios in severe bear markets and this is evident from the poor performances of equity mutual funds during prolonged bear markets, even though fund managers are highly experienced professionals.

One of the reasons for the inability of investors to exit is the phenomenon of their "getting married" to the stocks they own. Long term investors are especially prone to this pitfall. However, if an investor can work himself out of this defeatist strategy, then exiting the stock is the best hedge against a falling market is. Thus, for example, even a trailing stop loss of 25% as a defensive measure would provide a lot of protection to an investor.

What if the investor cannot bring himself to exit the stocks he owns? The only solution then is for him to hedge the portfolio by using futures and options. Hedging is an important tool, and one used by fund managers who are able to generate returns superior to Nifty from their portfolios.

Hedging by Buying Put Options

An at-the-money put option may have a premium of approximately 1% of Nifty value and will provide full protection against any downfall in Nifty prices. Out-of-the-money puts are cheaper but then they do not provide adequate protection. If full protection of portfolio is sought at all times then put options have to bought even when the trend is clearly up and thus there is an unnecessary, and preventable, erosion of portfolio returns due to premium paid for buying these puts. To avoid these unnecessary costs, put options can be bought only when a sell signal is generated by using a sound system based on technical analysis, such as the one propounded in this book.

Hedging by Selling Nifty Futures

Selling Nifty futures (or buying put options) on the basis of technical analysis is the only logical method of hedging since the use of fundamentals — such as a high P/E ratio or low dividend yield of the market — for hedging will often be at a huge cost. It is a well known fact that markets can remain overbought, in other words overvalued, for a long period of time. Consequently, selling based on overbought criteria, especially in a bull market, will often lead to losses. It is also important to understand the difference in the longevity of overbought and oversold situations. When a market gets overbought, few investors are actually in a hurry to exit their long positions owing to the well known "getting married to the stock" market phenomenon. An oversold market can, however, attract a lot of smart investors who had been waiting to buy at lower levels, rather quickly. That is why **markets do not remain oversold for long but can remain overbought for quite a long time.**

It is imperative, therefore, that before selling Nifty futures for hedging purposes, the investor must ensure that the higher level trend, namely the trend on the weekly charts, has shown indications of turning down. There are several methods for ascertaining this.

Much of traditional technical analysis is concerned with reversal signals such as head and shoulders formation, etc. Although selling based on such patterns may yield profits, there is no guarantee that market will oblige the investor by forming a clear cut reversal pattern.

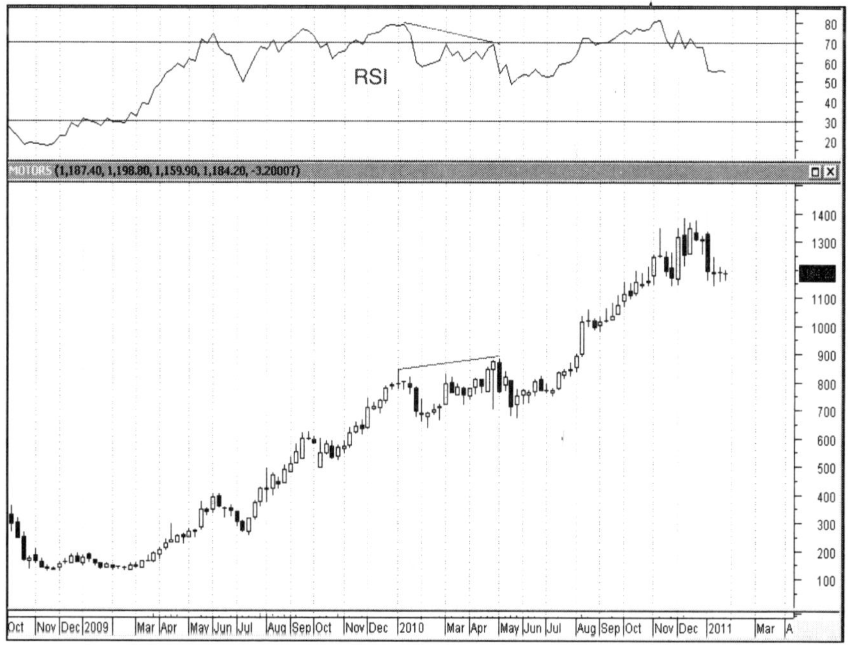

Figure 20.1: **Weekly chart of Tata Motors showing that the price staged a spectacular rise even after a negative divergence was seen in the 14-week RSI.**

~

Negative divergences between price and momentum are also often used to forecast the possibility of downside reversal but it may not be advisable to establish a big short position based only on such a divergence. Multiple negative divergences are often a feature of a raging bull market and no heed is paid to them by long term investors riding a roaring bull (*see* Figure 20.1).

Figure 20.2: **Weekly chart of Nifty showing that there was no evidence of any negative divergence when the savage bear market of 2008 began. The upper panel of the chart shows the 14-week RSI**

~

Figure 20.2 shows that even traditional technical analysis would have been useless as there were none of the price formations which are usually associated with bull market reversals, until far too late.

At the height of a bull market, the 13WMA line is above the 34WMA line, and the weekly MACD is in buy mode. The first indication of a reversal, as per the mechanical system outlined in this book, will be seen when the weekly MACD goes into sell mode. The exact manner of selling Nifty futures as a hedge is based upon the following parameters:

- Formation of an ROC based mechanical swing low once the weekly MACD goes into sell mode;

- Creation of a swing high thereafter; followed by a break of the previous swing low.

This is the earliest point where Nifty futures may be shorted. This is the contra-trend sell signal to be taken for hedging.

Once the 13WMA line goes below the 34WMA line, the longer term trend should then be considered as down and the investor must shift his focus to daily charts to look for overbought conditions, namely watch out for the 8DMA line going above the 21DMA line (*see* Figure 20.3). Once that happens, the

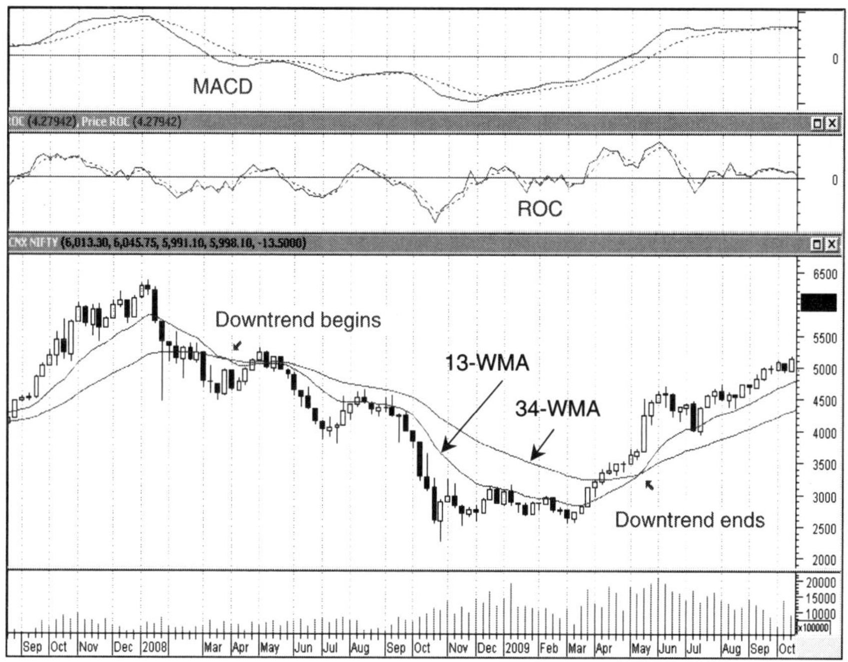

Figure 20.3: **Nifty's weekly chart showing the period of downtrend in Nifty from January 2008 till October 2008, highlighting the start and end points of the downward phase.**

~

short position can be established on the break of an ROC based mechanical swing low on the daily chart, as already explained in chapter 15. This is the pro-trend sell signal to be taken for hedging the portfolio.

Thus, from 4 April 2008 to 22 May 2009, the investor could have been short in Nifty whenever a safe opportunity became available (*see* Figure 20.4).

As highlighted in Figure 20.4, the first pro-trend short sale took place, on 26 May 2008, when Nifty broke the swing low of 4,914 established on 12 May. The stop loss would have been placed on the swing high of 5,167 which had been established on 16 May. The quantity in this trade should be decided by the size of the portfolio the investor would like to hedge. The trade was finally exited at 4,215, spanning a fall of 699 points.

Profit per share of Nifty = Sell price – Buy price

= 4,914 – 4,215 = 699

Profit in percentage terms = (699/4,914) X 100 = 14.2%

Hence, the profit in this trade was 14.20%.

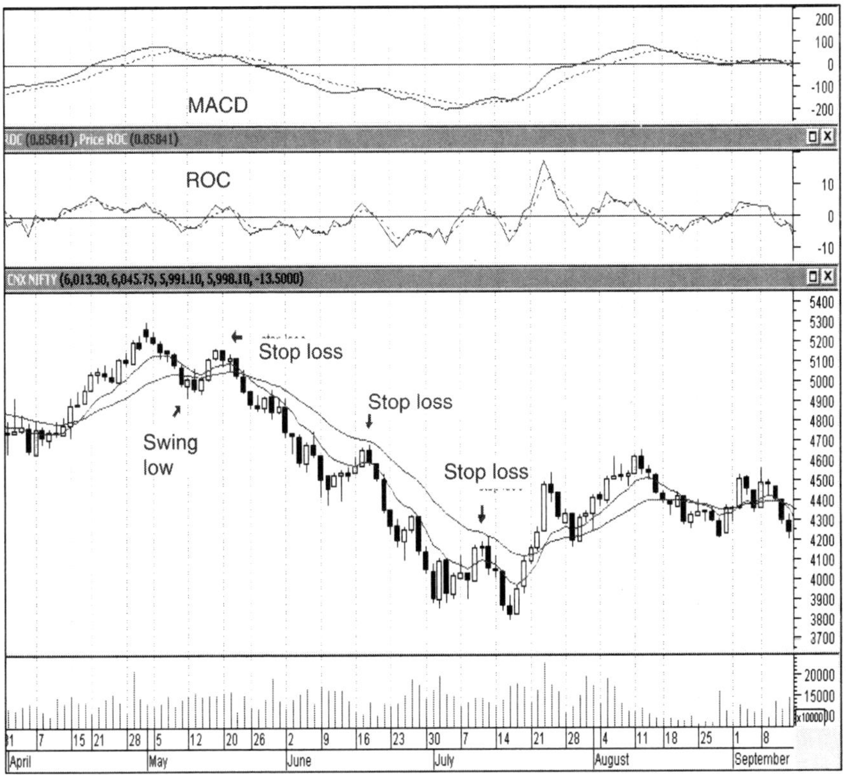

Figure 20.4: **Daily chart of Nifty showing the first pro-trend sell signal after the peak of 2003-2008 bull market.**

~

The investor would, of course, have suffered an almost similar, or bigger, loss on his investment portfolio but the profit earned by the short sale of Nifty futures would lessen the pain.

Importantly, such profits also provide additional capital at market bottoms when the investor may like to add a few more blue chips to his long term investment portfolio now available at lower prices.

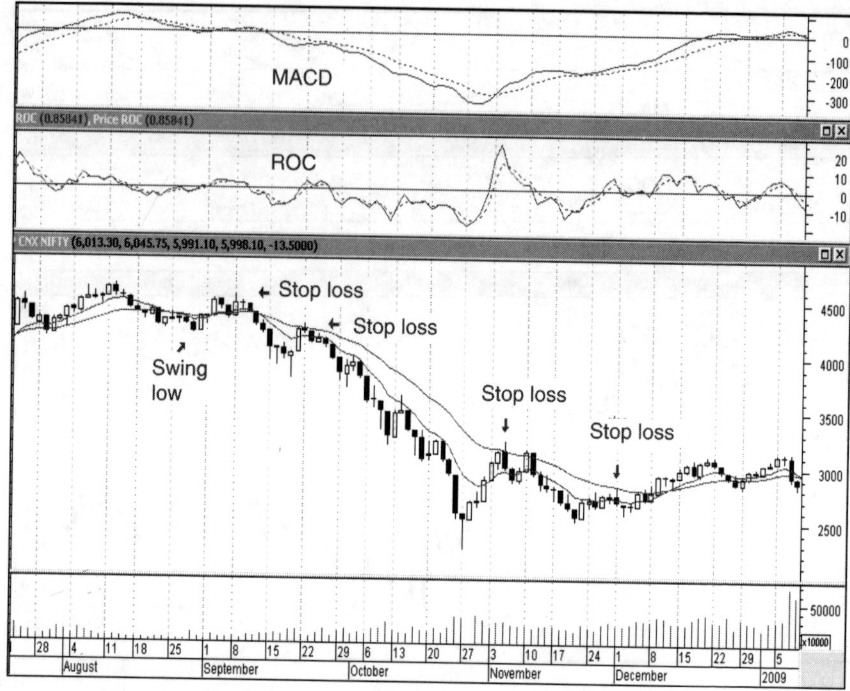

Figure 20.5: **The second pro-trend sell signal highlighted on Nifty's daily chart**

~

The chart in Figure 20.5 highlights the second short position that was established on the break of the swing low 4,202 (the low of 28 August) with a stop loss above the level of 4,558 — the swing high of 8 September. The trade was exited at 2,833 in January 2009, giving a profit of 1,369 points.

Profit per share of Nifty = Sell price – Buy price

= 4,202 – 2,833 = 1,371

Profit in percentage terms = (1,371 / 4,202) X100 = 32.62%

Thus, the profit in this trade was 32.62%.

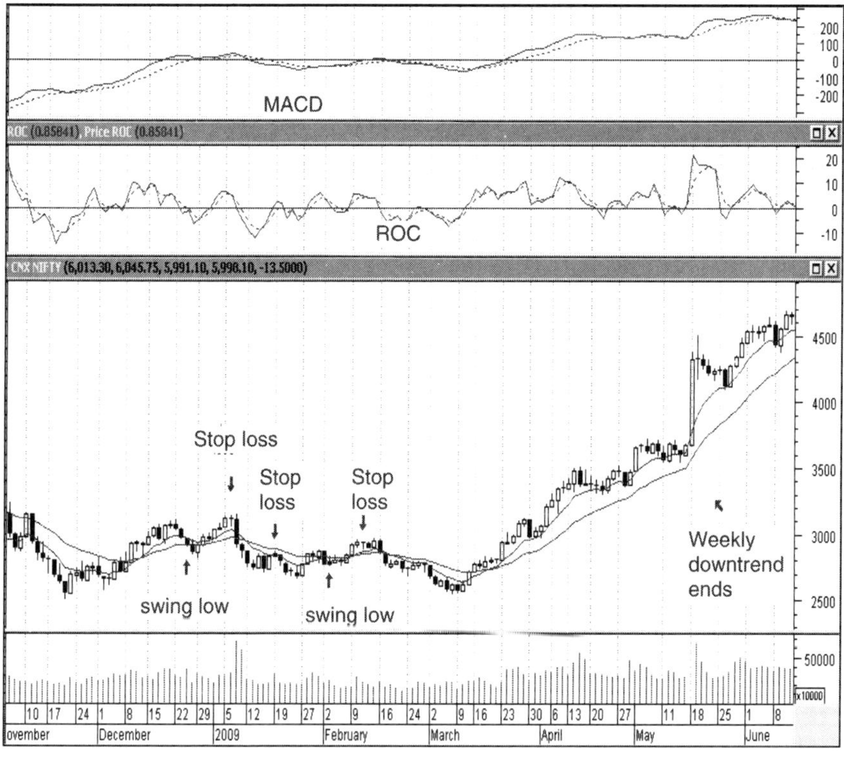

Figure 20.6: **The third and fourth sell signals highlighted on Nifty's daily chart.**

~

The third and fourth trades, shown in the chart in Figure 20.6, both resulted in losses of 1.96% and 7.87%, respectively. The longer term downtrend indicated by the weekly chart ended thereafter.

The net result was as follows:

The first trade	:	+ 14.20%
The second trade	:	+ 32.62%
The third trade	:	– 1.96%
The fourth trade	:	– 7.87%
Total	**:**	**+36.99%**

It is possible that the time period discussed above was especially profitable from a hedging perspective, in this case, short selling. But it is also clear from the above example that the strategy is quite effective in preventing a large erosion of equity in severe bear markets. The market had made a peak of 6,336 on 9 January 2008 and had started to fall steeply thereafter. It made a low of 2,228 on 27 October 2008. The last hedging signal would have been exited at a price of ₹2,974 on 24 March 2009. **During this period, a typical portfolio would have lost approximately 53% whereas our hedged portfolio would have only lost approximately 16%.**

How Much of Your Portfolio Should You Hedge

It is advisable to hedge the complete portfolio if time tested fundamentals such as interest rates are also turning against the market. It is very difficult, if not impossible, for stock markets to sustain an uptrend if interest rates rise handsomely. If investors can earn decent returns without assuming any risk, why would they bother to invest in the stock market and assume its related risks? **If an investor is in doubt regarding the direction of fundamentals, he may decide to hedge half of his portfolio.**

While taking a pro-trend sell signal, the full portfolio can be hedged without fear whereas only half of the portfolio should be hedged when taking a contra-trend sell signal. There is always some doubt about the direction of fundamentals affecting the market while taking a contra-trend signal (hence half the position) but there are no such doubts when the trend as shown by weekly chart is down and a pro-trend signal is being contemplated (hence a full position).

~

21

~

Relative Strength

Buy High, Sell Higher

Relative strength is a comparison of the relative performance of stocks and indices over a chosen period, and the strategies using this tool are based on the "Greater Fool Theory." Relative strength should be distinguished from relative strength index (RSI), which is an oscillator we've discussed earlier, and which we use in our mechanical trading system. Those buying stocks with superior relative performance are not always acting foolishly.

To calculate the relative strength of a stock, the stock's price is compared to that of an index; in this case, say Nifty. The resultant curve will show whether the relative strength of the stock is falling or rising*. The strategies using relative strength are based on the hypothesis that there is always a "greater fool" to whom the stock can be sold at a higher price. Indeed, it is a fact that the momentum of the stock can be relied upon to take it a little bit

* You would remember that relative strength index (RSI), on the other hand, is calculated by using previous prices of the stock itself, without making any comparison with index values.

further. **Though not of much use to a long term investor, there is sufficient empirical evidence that relative strength is an excellent tool for forecasting short term price performance and can be used for selecting stocks which are more likely to show a trending pattern.** The major obstacle is that if the trader fails to find a greater fool than himself, he may be unable to sell the stock at a higher price and the stock may, in fact, be ripe for a dramatic reversal to the downside.

By its very nature, relative strength encourages the trader to buy stocks that have been rising for a relatively long period, and thus are usually overbought at the time when they appear as best performers on the charts. Clearly, then, it is not advisable to buy such overbought stocks for long term investment as most of the good story may have already been discounted. On the other hand, it is also a well known phenomenon that a stock can remain in overbought territory for a quite long time due to the tendency of investors of "getting married to the stock." Hence, such stocks may either well be ready to enter a bear market or they may, more likely, continue making higher tops for a while longer. If a long position is created without having any sort of stop loss then the trader is taking the risk of a rather large loss.

Since most stocks are more volatile than Nifty, the chances of false breakdowns of stop loss levels are quite high. Even if the actual stop loss is placed at a distance of 1% from the estimated stop loss, it may be hit and, thereafter, the price may reverse itself from there and go on to make new highs.

There are two alternatives for dealing in individual stocks that are stronger than Nifty:

1. Buy the selected stock on the basis of its own chart.

2. Buy the selected stocks as a basket when a buy signal is received on the Nifty chart.

The first of these approaches is time consuming but may be suitable for some traders. The advantage is that it provides well defined individual stop losses. Of course, the trader should be careful to avoid stocks with low liquidity.

The second approach is rather easy to follow but, occasionally, the loss in a particular stock can be quite large due to adverse events and hence it is recommended that a trailing stop loss of maximum 10% must be placed on the stock, below the highest closing price reached after making the entry in the case of long positions, and *vice versa* in the case of short positions.

Weak stocks can, similarly, be selected as short sale candidates.

Three important factors to remember while selecting such stocks are:

1. The stocks selected must be from different sectors.

2. A minimum of four stocks must be sold or bought whenever a signal is received in Nifty. This will diversify the portfolio adequately and avoid any major unpleasant surprises.

3. The investment in each of the four stocks must be equal. This may be a little difficult to achieve in practice because of the differences in value of the contracts among different stocks. For example, in 2018 a single contract of Infosys was worth ₹8 lakh while that of Tata Motors was worth ₹3 lakh. This can be managed if the minimum investment in each stock is kept at, say, ₹10 lakh. Due to the fixed lot size provision, the investor will have to buy a different number of lots for different stocks and will generally be able to have an investment of ₹9 to ₹11 lakh in each. This difference is minor and will not disturb the overall returns to any large extent.

Stocks may be selected on the basis of their 12-month performance in relation to Nifty. It is advised that the trader conduct his own research and work out the relevant time period to his own satisfaction.

There is no doubt that the returns are better than Nifty with such an approach but the risk is also greater and hence the risk and reward ratio of trading on the basis of relative strength may not really be better than that from trading Nifty on the basis of a proven and profitable strategy. Furthermore, the margin requirements in individual stocks are also higher than in Nifty. This kind of basket trading may be more suitable for those using moving average crossovers in their strategy. For example, if 8DMA of Nifty futures goes above 13DMA, then buy a basket of strong stocks. When the opposite crossover occurs, exit the strong stocks and short sell a basket of weak stocks. This will allow the trader to be always in the market. It is strongly emphasized that you conduct a thorough research if you intend to use such an approach in your trading.

~

22 ~ Intraday Trading, Anyone?

Intraday trading, or day trading, is one area which even professionals traders are apprehensive of entering. This form of trading requires very strict discipline. Also, brokerage and slippages constitute a large part of the cost of intraday trading. The trader must close his trade either before or at the end of the day to be a true intraday trader, even if holding it overnight may have been more profitable.

For example, if a trading system, such as the swing breakouts we have described earlier, is applied to intraday charts, and if an opposing signal is not received by the end of the day then the position has to be exited prematurely.

Traders could, however, consider using smaller time frame charts, namely 5- or 15-minute charts for intraday trading using our system, but they must first conduct a thorough study of the past data to validate any conclusions.

As we have already seen, the business of trading is crucially dependent on discipline, and most brokers will tell you that more than 95% of traders quit trading within one year, to be replaced by a new set of hopefuls. Although faulty methods of entry, exits and money management may also be the reasons, the most common reason is, usually the inability to strictly follow their own methods, which is what leads traders to ruin. While the same tactics need to be applied on intraday basis, the constant stress of the trading environment may be such as to completely overwhelm the trader, preventing any chance of noteworthy success. Even though exposure to the kind of short term trading system outlined in Chapter 18 also requires the trader's attentive engagement during trading hours but the trade can, at least, be carried to next day.

In sum: stay away from intraday trading till you develop sufficient experience, and, above all, great self discipline and equanimity.

~

23

~

Trading Forex and Commodities

One of the beauties of technical analysis is that once you get a grasp of the subject, you can use it to trade any and every security or financial instrument which is freely traded in the market place, and whose prices are governed by demand and supply.

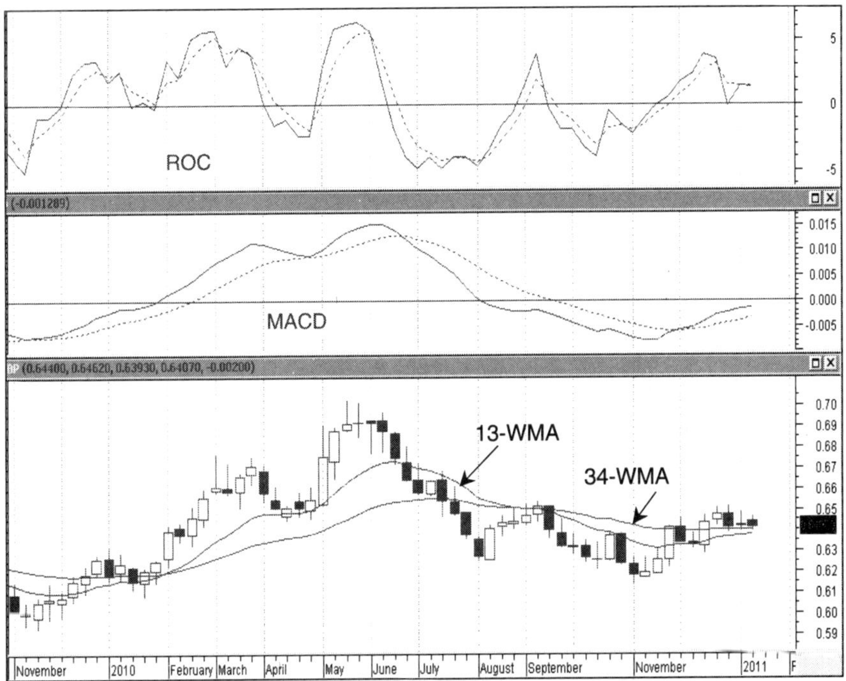

Figure 23.1: **Weekly chart of USDGBP (US Dollar *versus* Great British Pound)**

~

Figure 23.1 shows that the trend of USDGBP (US dollar *versus* Great British Pound) as indicated by the weekly chart was up from February 2010 to August 2010. After making a peak of 0.70 on 21 May 2010, the USDGBP started falling.

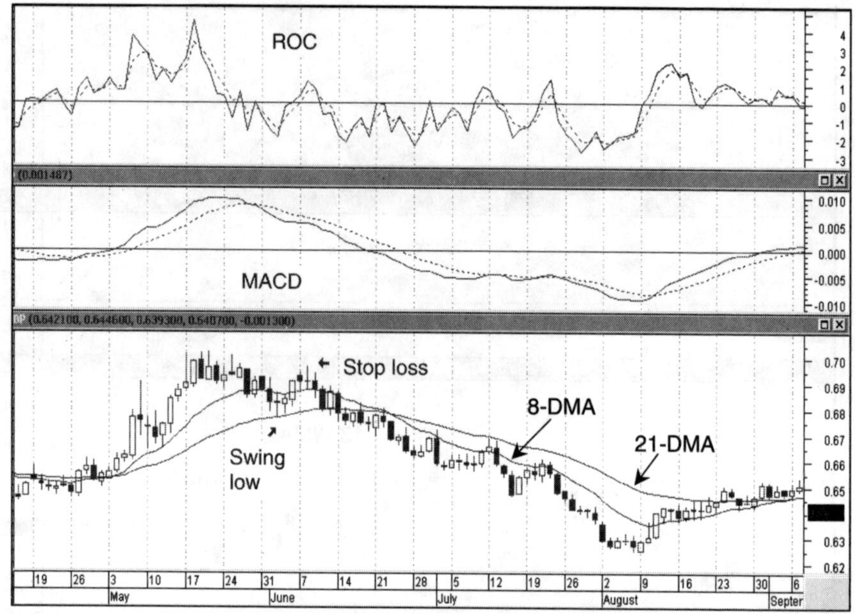

Figure 23.2: **Daily chart of USDGBP**

~

Figure 23.2 shows the daily chart of USDGBP. As per our system, a contra-trend sell signal was generated when the price broke the swing low of 0.68 on 14 June 2010. The trade would have been finally exited in December of that year when the trailing stop loss of 0.64 was hit.

The profit generated in this trade was 5.9% without the use of margin. Margin requirements in foreign exchange contracts are usually less than 10% and the actual profit on capital deployed would have been in excess of 59%.

~

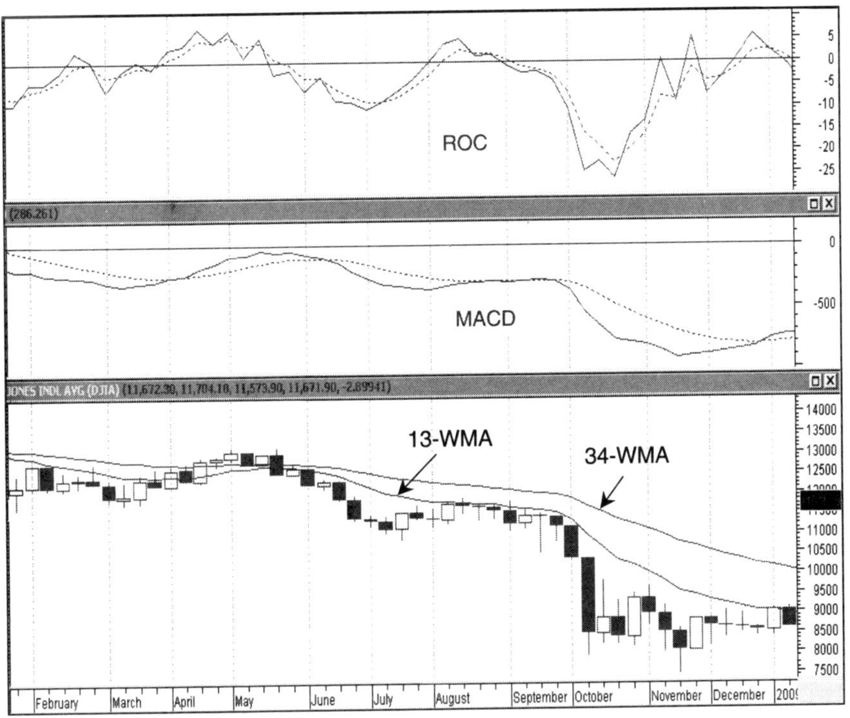

Figure 23.3: **Weekly chart of Dow Jones Industrial Average (DJIA) showing a downtrend in force in 2008**

~

Figure 23.3 is a weekly chart of Dow Jones Industrial Average (DJIA). A downtrend was seen in force in 2008. A trader using our system would have looked to establish a short position on some evidence of upward correction in the daily chart.

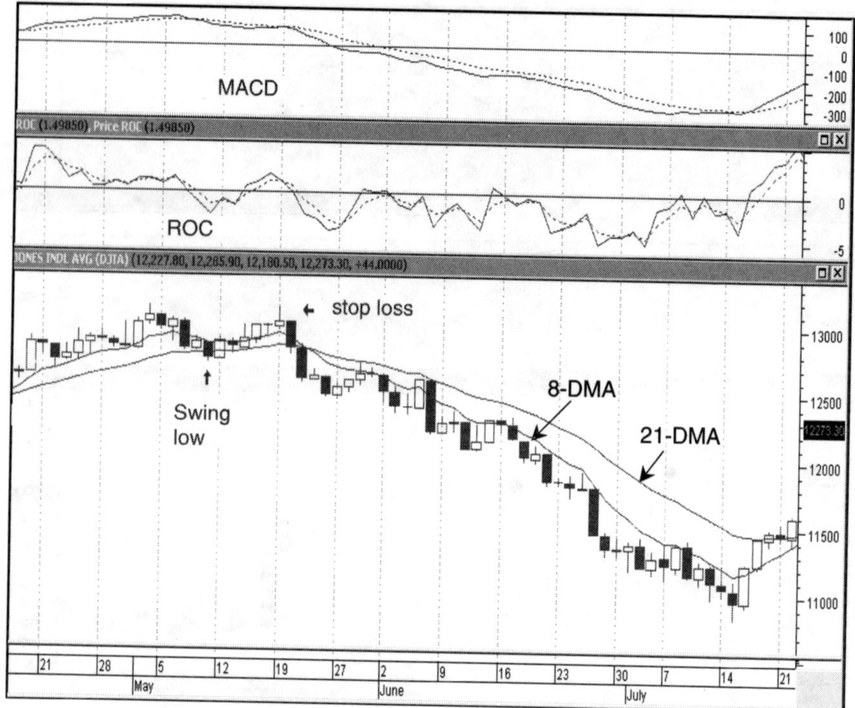

Figure 23.4: **Daily chart of DJIA in May 2008, with a short trade highlighted**

~

The daily chart of DJIA in Figure 23.4 shows that the 8DMA line went above the 21DMA line and trader could have gone short on the break of the swing low of 9 May at the level of 12,715. A nice downtrend ensued thereafter. The trade would have finally been exited at the level of 11,698, generating a profit of 8%, again without using any margin.

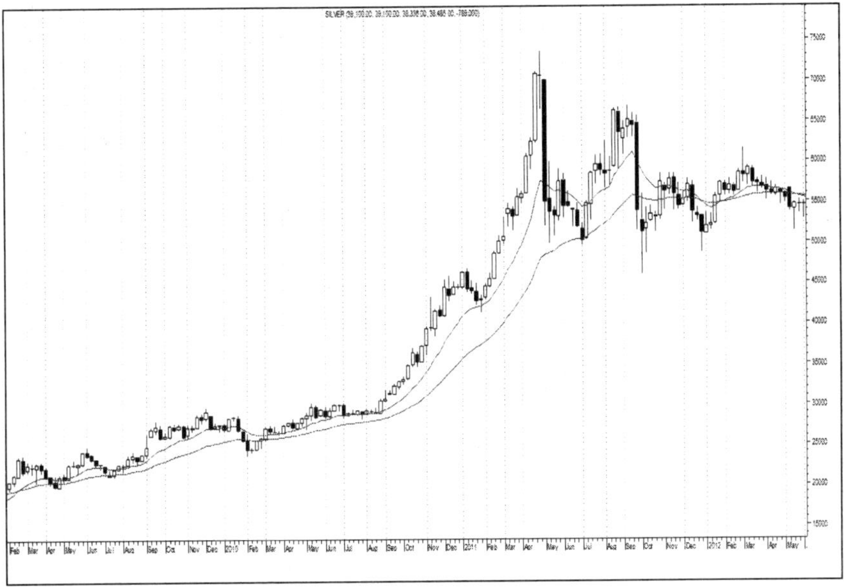

Figure 23.5: **Weekly chart of silver, which was in an uptrend since the beginning of 2009**

~

The weekly trend of silver was up since the beginning of 2009, as shown in the chart in Figure 23.5. A trader should have been looking to buy on evidence of downward corrections on the daily chart.

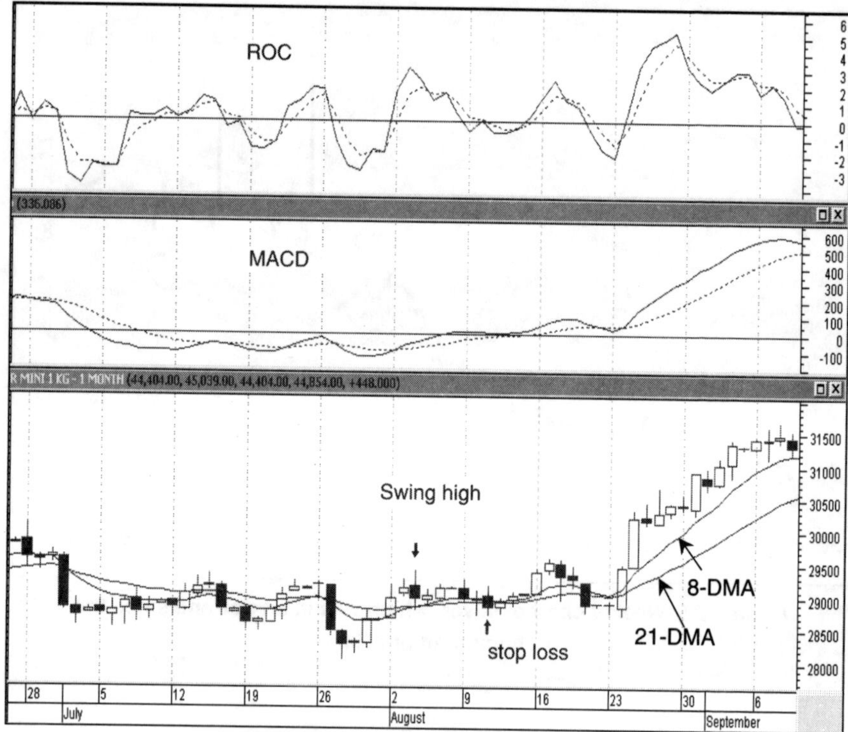

Figure 23.6: **Daily chart of silver in August 2010, with the long trade highlighted**

~

As per our system, the uptrend in silver should have been entered into at the level of ₹29,390 in August 2010. The trade is highlighted in the daily chart of silver in Figure 23.6. That trade progressed satisfactorily till its exit signal in January 2011 at the level of 43,550 as shown in Figures 23.6 and 23.7.

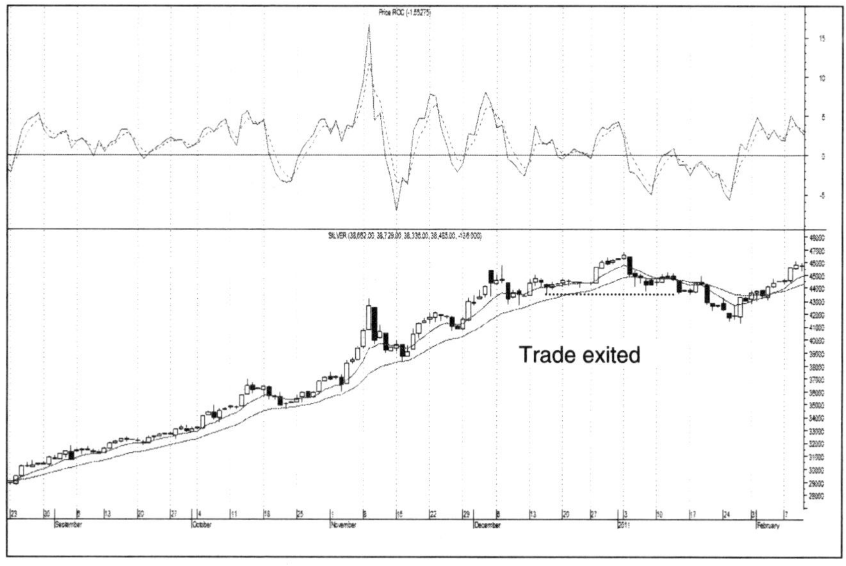

Figure 23.7: **The long silver trade was exited in January 2011**

~

The examples given above demonstrate that our trading system can be used with confidence in any instrument which is freely traded in the markets and which has some sort of speculating element in it. Trading in silver, foreign currencies, agricultural items or metals may be suitable for meeting hedging requirements of those who are exposed to such risks on a day to day basis. They may also be suitable for a trader with large capital at his disposal since diversification through uncorrelated assets helps in reducing the overall risk of trading.

~

24

~

Some Other Considerations

Changing the Trading System

It is possible that even after applying strict discipline and stringent money management techniques, you are unable to get the trading results you desire. This may be due to some unarticulated expectations of yours which the system you are using is unable to fulfill. For example, such an expectation may be in the form of a desire that you want your first trade itself to be profitable, or an expectation that you would be lucky enough to escape the rigors of the learning curve.

To deal with this possibility, ask yourself the following questions:

- Did you research the system before you started using it?
- What was the duration of your research?
- What was the maximum number of loss-making trades in a row?
- Was there any unusual event, such as the market opening with a huge gap against your trading position, during the trial pe-

riod, which might have given a larger than expected loss and which may be treated as a one-off event?

- Did you research the new system thoroughly before replacing an existing one?
- Does it require any subjective input?
- Is it simpler, or more complicated, than the previous system?
- Does your new system require averaging against the trend? Such a system may show profits in the short run but has the potential to ultimately ruin the trader.

In short, a trader should not initiate trading based upon an unproven system. On the other hand, once adopted s/he should not then abandon a system before it has had sufficient time to perform.

Diversification

Diversification is considered a most important safeguard against losses. This may be true when you are investing rather than trading. In trading, the major risk comes from your trading system and your inability to follow the system rigorously. If you are trading four or five different stocks on a continuous basis, your losses in one may be temporarily compensated by gains in another stock, but the ultimate profitability from each single item is a function of the accuracy of your trading system. Furthermore, many traders do not have sufficient time available for analyzing so many stocks and so a lack of diversification should not be considered a barrier to trading in the stock markets.

The point that is being made here is that it is not an all or none situation; namely, if you want to trade successfully, you have either to be diversified, or you should not trade at all. A beginning can be made with one item and a diversified trading portfolio can be built slowly as experience, knowledge and profits accumulate.

As highlighted in Chapter 10, a trader should not risk more than 2% of his capital on any single trade. Furthermore, the trader should not hold more than 5 positions at any one time so that the total risk to his capital is never more than 10%. Now, if the trader has only ₹5 lakh at his disposal, the maximum risk allowed in one trade is ₹10,000. This amount is not adequate to trade on the basis of daily charts since the stop loss on his position may be 200 to 300 points away and the minimum risk required to hold one contract of Nifty may be ₹15,000 to ₹22,500 as one contract of Nifty is made up of 75 units at the time of this writing. Either the trader has to increase his risk per trade — not recommended — or he may need to raise additional capital, which may not be possible. An alternative is to trade smaller time frame charts, e.g. 15-minute charts, where the stop loss usually is not more than 50 points away. The trader can then afford to trade in 2 to 3 contracts of Nifty futures.

However, In case adequate capital is available then a trader must diversify his risk in four to five different securities. As far as possible, these items should not have any correlation with one another, which means that factors which affect the movements of one security should have no effect on the other items. Such items may be a mix of stock index futures, agricultural items, metals, foreign exchanges or bonds, etc. Unfortunately, there are some practical difficulties in creating such a trading portfolio. Trading in metals continues till midnight. Agricultural items do not provide adequate liquidity. Trading in bonds is almost non-existent in India for the individual trader. Hence, a compromise can be made by trading in Nifty, Bank Nifty and 2 to 3 stock futures selected from different sectors.

Managing Surplus Funds

Most strategies given in this book require a rather discontinuous flow of funds. For example, if you are trading in Nifty futures on the basis of the daily chart, and your position size is based on a fixed amount of risk per trade, then you will:

1. Require different amounts of margin for different trades based on their position size.
2. Require a surplus amount to meet the losses and continue trading.

As shown in Chapter 17, you may require up to ₹25 lakh of trading capital if you are planning to assume a risk of ₹50,000 per trade. A part of this amount would need to be kept with the broker to meet margin requirements.

If the available capital is less than that, the risk amount should be reduced proportionately. It is recommended that initially you trade only in Nifty futures as this would require a smaller capital. For example, for a risk per trade of ₹50,000, the actual capital required (at the time of this writing) would not be more than ₹5 lakh. This, however, means that the trader would be risking 10% of his capital on a Nifty trade alone. Hence, it is vital that even though ₹5 lakh are adequate to trade in Nifty, the trader must have at least ₹25 lakh and the amount of ₹5 lakh should be considered only a segment of the total capital of ₹25 lakh. This doesn't, however, mean that trading is not possible with smaller capital. The only requirement would be that the trader would have to trade in smaller time frames to reduce the risk per trade accordingly.

You also have the option of parking the required capital in a liquid fund or you could get a fixed deposit receipt from the bank. In the latter case, you should open an overdraft facility with the bank and draw money from this account to meet the losses. Some brokers also provide the facility to make fixed deposits in banks on behalf of their clients and consider these deposits to be in the nature of margin money. The interest earned on those deposits is credited to the client's account. Furthermore, if you have a portfolio of stocks in your demat account, the broker may also treat these stocks as collaterals for margin money requirements. Mark-to-market losses, of course, have to be paid on a day to day basis. Occasionally, the market may open with a large gap against one's position and a large mark to market loss may be there. If such a loss is within the assumed risk, it should be of no consideration but if it is beyond that, then the trader will be required to bring additional cash. There is however, no need to worry unduly about gap openings since an adequately diversified portfolio will often be able to prevent large losses. You should discuss all these issues with your broker and try to get the maximum benefit in this regard. Also, try to get a broker with the lowest brokerage rates.

~

25

~

Why I am Sharing My Trading System with You

Why should I share my trading system with everyone instead of using it to make money only for myself? It seems you have caught me on the wrong foot here. Or, may be not.

Firstly, I am making money using the system described in this book. My income from trading has freed me from the worries of my medical practice. Although I had quite busy practice, I found the medical profession fast degenerating into a low income, high stress job. The ever increasing expectations of patients in a highly competitive environment led to a situation where I was working from 8 A.M. to 9 P.M. with hardly any break in between. Even Sundays were no holidays for me. The pressures of the profession were such that sometimes I could not even attend to my own sick family members. It was with great difficulty that I was able to have a week's holiday in a year with my family. **Now that my trading income has surpassed my income from medical profession, what was a highly stressful medical practice has become a pleasant affair.** I have been able to raise my professional fees and curtail the consultation timings. I am enjoying my vacations and am also able to spend time with my family. That is what I had aimed for, and expected from, trading.

Secondly, does it really matter whether I give you my best system or not? Consider the following two alternative scenarios.

Suppose I have given you the very best system I know as of now. After finishing this book, and with slight experience, you will soon realize that having a good system — or even the best system in the world — is only one of the factors which determine your trading success. You also need soldier-like discipline, coupled with a high degree of detachment from your trading results. These two qualities, namely discipline and mastery over your emotions, are not easy to come by. It is one thing to be disciplined in a profession where the reward is directly proportional to your labor, i.e. you will get nothing if you don't work but you don't have to pay from your pocket for not working — and another thing to remain disciplined in a profession where your actions could even lead to losses. It will take at least two to three years for you to understand the value of discipline in trading. The other quality, namely detachment, is perhaps one of the toughest goals one can aspire to in one's life time. It was the cornerstone of Lord Krishna's philosophy and what he taught Arjun in the battle of Mahabharat. Arjun, of course, went on to win the war. When you win the war of trading, rest assured that you will win it because of your determination and emotional control, and my system will be a very insignificant part of your success. That is why I have no problem in sharing my successful system with you.

Now suppose I am not giving you my best system? Or, maybe I am giving you the worst system I have ever developed? Should this be a cause of worry for you? Not at all! That's because you must not apply any system without independent research of your own. If you do so, you will have hardly any confidence even in the best of systems. If after your research, on the other hand, you find that my system is defective then your studies would have yielded you several alternatives. You can then make modifications in this system, or maybe develop your own system. My system, then, is only the starting point for you.

I am going to share a personal communication I was proud to receive from Tony Plummer to further highlight this point.

> Dear Dr. Vijay Gupta,
>
> As you have found out, however, books are only a beginning: The real work comes in developing your own way of being with new ideas and then building on them. In trading, quite obviously, this means developing your own systems — ones that really work for you and that you always trust. Even when the signals don't give you a financial profit, if you have a good stop loss, then you can try again. The art is always to preserve capital.
>
> The late Joseph Campbell used to advise people to "follow your bliss." When you know yourself well, then feeling good about doing something is the surest sign that you have that you are doing the right thing.
>
> Tony Plummer
>
> 27 October 2005

~

I have been using the system described in this book for nearly fifteen years now with a great degree of success but I do not claim it to be the best system in the world. Please derive your own conclusions.

26

~

Why My System is the Best

Learned readers of this book may be protesting at my not having mentioned many of the time honored theories and practices while describing the system being propounded in this book. An explanation is required regarding their place in our trading system, and what is it that makes me think that this system is the best.

One of the purposes of a mechanical system is to take the speculative element out of trading. Many people erroneously consider speculation and trading to be almost similar activities. That's simply not true. Speculation has been defined by John Maynard Keynes as "the activity of forecasting the psychology of the market" and its motive as "the object of securing profit from knowing better than the market what the future will bring." Speculators indulge in prediction-based trading but traders may not need predictions to sustain in business. Speculation is more focused on chance; trading is more focused on skill. In this manner, speculation is actually linked more to investment than trading. Think of that! A mechanical trading system of entries and exits, on the other hand, is not dependent upon estimations of future probability based on conjectures but on risk management by using statistically proven methods.

A mechanical system is also one which does not change due to circumstances external to the system. It is sometimes advised that a trader needs some perspective into the macro fundamentals to be successful and should correlate the signals from his mechanical system with such information. This, however, is not true. As we have already discussed elsewhere, it is impossible to know all the fundamentals affecting the market at any given time. To be a true fundamentalist, then, one needs the "mind of God," as Cynthia Case writes in her book, *Trading with the Odds*. Even if we concede that what is meant by perspectives is not fundamental information but technical analysis beyond what is incorporated in the system, the final outcome of speculating on these extraneous data, and then changing the management of an ongoing trade accordingly, will be detrimental to profits. Nevertheless, if some way can be found to make a permanent change in the system itself on the basis of some proven theory of technical analysis, the results could then be highly encouraging. The only caveat here is whether such a change will also result in the system getting so complicated that it may become difficult to use in practice. Hence the trade-off is between higher profitability and usefulness.

Further, except for moving average crossovers and similar other methods, there is no system of technical analysis which will catch every trade. In the case of moving average crossovers, though the signal may catch all the trades, it works successfully only in trending markets. The drawdowns can be huge in choppy markets and the risk reward ratio may also not be favorable. Those systems which filter out some trades on the basis of low probability of success will, occasionally, filter out some highly profitable ones, too. The aim of the trader is to make money and not to rue on what he could have made, as long as he is getting a just reward for his efforts.

Traders can end up developing profitable systems as well as losing systems. A losing system can be the outcome of a lack of knowledge. Lack of knowledge, however, is only one of the factors. A more common factor is a wrong estimation of one's own risk taking capacity. If a system seems to be giving frequent small profits but an occasional large loss, it may still be considered useful by the trader since he may feel that the occasional losing trade will not occur in the near future. But what if the very first trade itself is a loss-making one? If the system is designed to enable early entries and exits, then numerous whipsaws may cause the trader to feel frustrated. In case the system is able to filter out a lot of bad trades, then the entry and exit prices may not be favorable in the sense that price may have already moved a long way from the base, or the top, before any entry or exit signal is generated. In other words, one has to choose between specificity and sensitivity. For example, in the system being propounded in this book if one tries to establish a long position before the mechanical swing has given a breakout, then the signal may prove to be false and generate a loss. However, there will be occasions when the same tactic will prove profitable as well.

How many types of signals can one take in a given system? Consider, for example, the following four types of buy signals that Tony Plummer has suggested in his system:

1. A contra-trend buy or sell signal which is entered after evidence of positive or negative divergence is seen on the charts.
2. A pro-trend buy or sell signal which is entered after a correction.
3. A buy or sell signal which is entered due to a signal from traditional technical analysis.
4. A buy or sell signal which is entered on the evidence of a Fibonacci retracement.

What would happen if a trader follows only one type of signal from among these four types? The point is that all these signals are independently profitable and, hence, the profitability of one is not dependent upon the others, but a combined use of all four together may result in lower drawdowns. If, for example, only a contra-trend sell signal is taken, and it results in a loss, but the consecutive pro-trend buy signal, which may have been profitable, is not taken, then it may be a long time before another contra-trend sell signal is received. The purpose of a complete system is to improve the probabilities but a trader has to assess whether he has the wherewithal or, to put it simply, guts, to withstand the rigors of such a system. In that sense, the best system for a trader is the one which he is also comfortable with. One need not look for some universally "best" system.

So far as I'm concerned, it's my confidence in my system that makes it the best system in the world.

Even then, no system will be able to generate confidence unless it can withstand scrutiny from established theories of technical analysis and we shall now make an effort to benchmark the strength and weaknesses of our system by this yardstick.

Dow Theory

Promulgated by Charles H. Dow in early twentieth century, the Dow Theory has been an extremely popular bedrock of technical analysis ever since. The theory is based upon the construction of two averages, namely the Dow Jones Industrial Average (DJIA) and the Dow Jones Transportation Average (DJTA). The originator of the theory likened the movements of the stock market to those of the tides, waves, and ripples in the sea. The basic tenets of the theory are as follows:

1. The averages (indices) discount everything, except "acts of God."

2. There are three trends in the market; primary, secondary and minor (tertiary).
3. The primary trend is the major trend.
4. The secondary trends are corrections within the primary trend.
5. The minor (tertiary) trends are small day-to-day fluctuations, or noise, which are not of much significance.
6. A bull market primary trend can be divided into three phases, namely accumulation, a reasonably steady advance, and a speculative bubble in the last phase.
7. A bear market starts with the distribution phase, goes into the panic phase and, then, finally, into distress selling by those who have to raise cash for other needs.
8. The two averages (indices) must confirm.
9. Volume goes with the trend. An increase in volume when the prices are rising is used as a confirmation of an uptrend. If the volume decreases while the prices are still rising, it may indicate distribution and signal the possibility of market going down.
10. Lines may substitute for secondaries, namely the secondary correction may be sideway.
11. Only closing prices are significant.
12. A trend should be assumed to be in effect till such time as its reversal has been definitely signaled.

Based upon the Dow Theory, several methods of forecasting future prices have been developed which can together be thought of as traditional technical analysis. There are two broad categories of such methods:

1. **Reversal patterns**, such as head and shoulders, rounding top or bottom, broadening formations, etc. The head and shoulders is the most easily recognizable pattern and has a very high level of accuracy.

2. **Continuation patterns**, or consolidation formations, such as triangles, flags and wedges.

There is no denying that substantial profits can be made by using these methods in a proper manner. However, if one is using the system propounded in this book, there is no need to take these patterns into consideration because, on most occasions, you would be taking advantage of the patterns without explicitly following them. Let's see how.

Head and Shoulders Pattern

The inverted head and shoulders pattern shown in Figure 26.1 would have been good for initiating a long position when the price broke out of the neckline after forming the right shoulder.

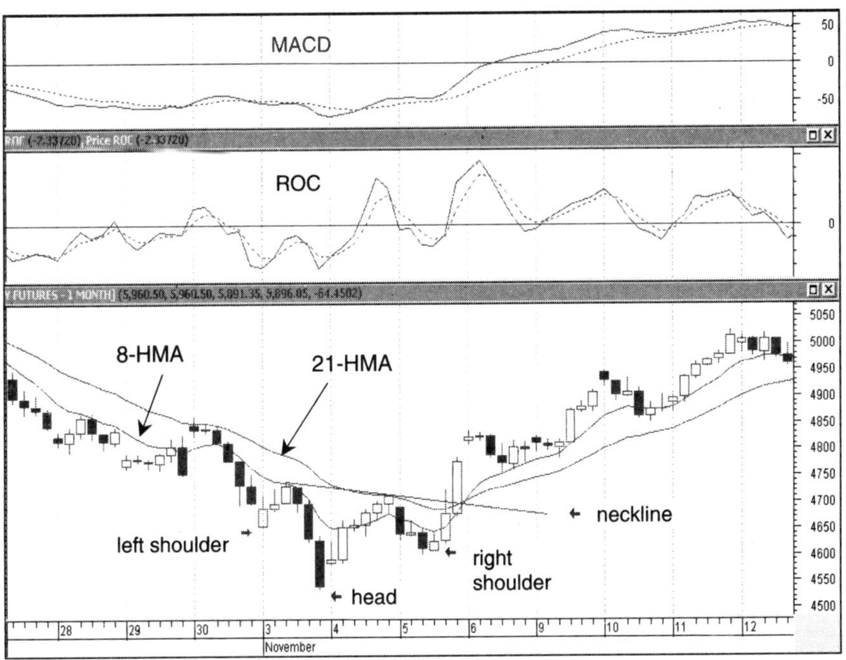

Figure 26.1: **Hourly chart of Nifty futures in October-November 2009 showing an inverted head and shoulders pattern**

~

The neckline then stood at 4,695. However, a trader using the method given in this book would have noticed that the 8HMA line (an 8-hourly moving average) was below the 21HMA line at this time, and the hourly MACD had gone into buy mode.

Furthermore, the daily trend (not shown in the chart in Figure 26.1) was down at this point, i.e. the 13DMA line was below 34DMA line. According to our contra-trend buy rule in a down-trend, the trader would have taken a long position when the price broke out of the swing high of 4 November at the level of 4,712 (*see* Figure 26.2).

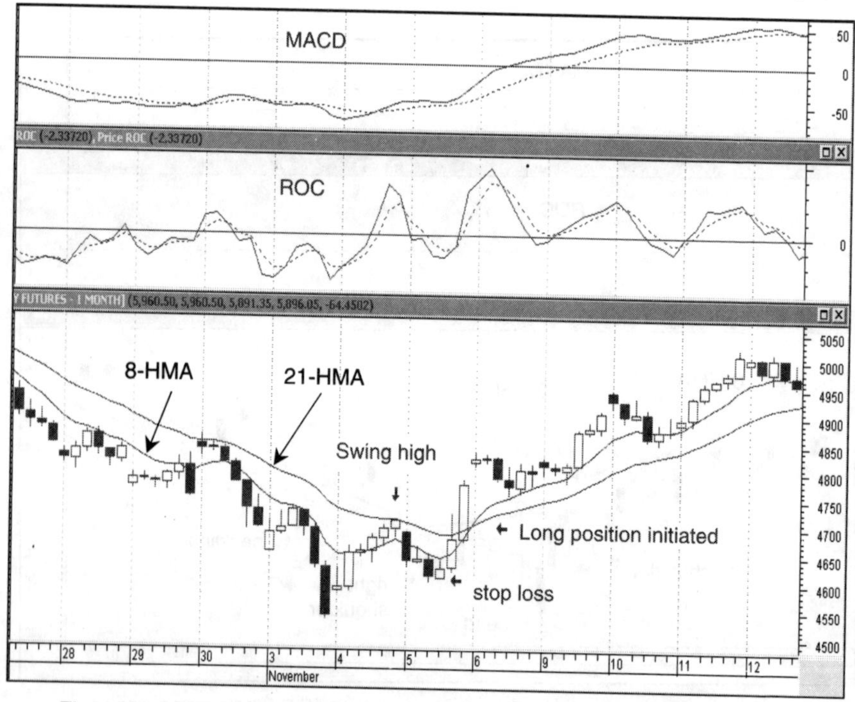

Figure 26.2: **Hourly chart of Nifty futures showing corresponding swing high and lows for entering into a long position**

~

This trade would have been exited at 5,006 at a profit of 294 points (6.2% profit without using any margin).

Figure 26.3 shows that after making a high of 2,171 in March 2005, Nifty started falling and reached a low of 1,877 in May. There was no reversal pattern visible at this point that would signal a resumption of the uptrend. However, the 13WMA line was above the 34WMA line during this period (not shown in the chart), and using the method given in this book, the trader would have observed that the 8DMA line was below the 21DMA line and, hence, a long position is to be entered when the swing high of 1,964 established on 25 April is broken on the upside.

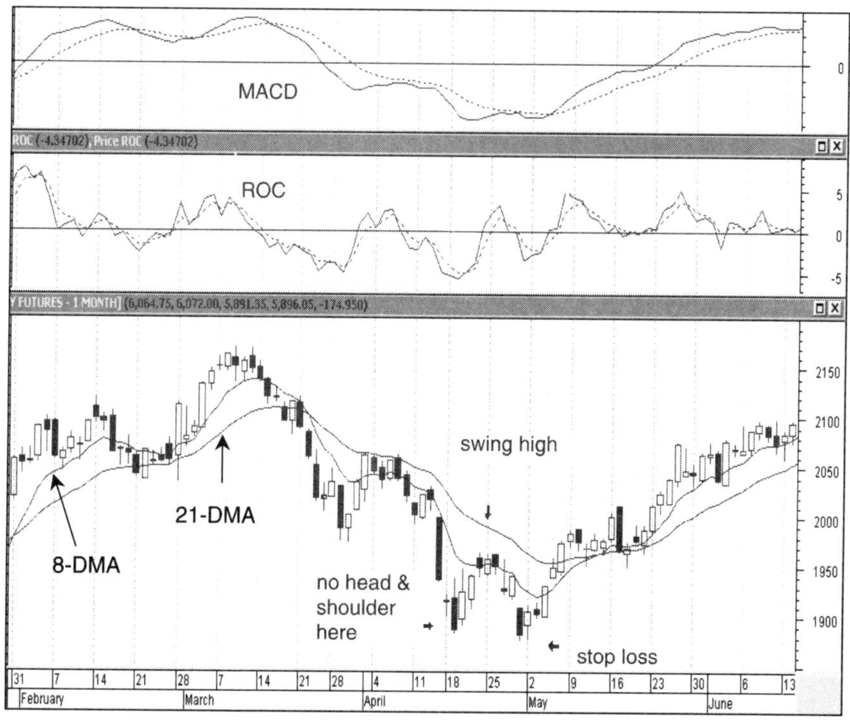

Figure 26.3: **Daily chart of Nifty futures in April-May 2005**

As stated earlier, there is no system which is perfect and the system given in this book is no exception. But the advantages of using a mechanical approach over a subjective approach should not be underestimated. The above mentioned trade was finally exited at 2,451 with a profit of 487 points, i.e. with a profit of 24.8% without using margin.

Continuation patterns can also be traded in the same manner. These patterns signify a correction in an ongoing up or down-trend. As per our system, an uptrend is almost always characterized by the 13WMA line being above the 34WMA line, and any significant minor correction will take the 8DMA line below the 21DMA line, thereby providing an entry point to the trader. In this way, when a flag is getting formed in a higher time frame, the trader can enter the trade in the lower time frame at a very attractive price.

Trend Lines

An uptrend line is the straight line drawn by joining successive troughs (bottoms) in a rising market, while a downtrend line is the straight line drawn by joining successive peaks (tops) in a falling market. A definitive buy signal is given when the price penetrates a downtrend line — or *vice versa*.

A valid trend line should possess the following features:

1. The line should touch at least three successive bottoms, or peaks, as the case may be.
2. The price should bounce back at least twice from the return line, which is drawn parallel to the trend line.
3. A trend line with an angle of 30 to 45 degrees is more likely to be valid than steeper lines.

Figure 26.4: **Daily chart of Nifty futures showing how the uptrend line was broken on the downside on 28 July 2010**

~

Figure 26.4 shows that an uptrend line in Nifty was broken on the downside on 28 July 2010, thereby triggering a short sale as well as exit from the long position. Purely on the basis of trend lines, however, one would have found it difficult to go long when the subsequent rally started in early September the same year.

Furthermore, those using the daily time frame chart to gauge the direction of the trend would have concluded that the trend had reversed downwards once the trend line was broken. However, the use of 13DMA and 34DMA line crossover as a trend determinant suggested that an uptrend was still in progress in the daily chart. Use of moving averages would have prevented many loss making short sales, on 60-minutes and 15-minutes charts, which would have been the case if trend line had been used instead for determining the trend. As explained earlier, for short term trades taken on the basis of 60-minute or 15-minute charts, the trend is determined by the daily chart.

One of the difficulties in using trend lines instead of moving averages is that these lines can be highly subjective. If the trader is anticipating a bullish move, he may well be tempted to draw a line which would justify his original view. This will not be the case if moving averages are used instead. Furthermore, if entry and exits are based on trend line breaks, then the results of such a system are unlikely to be very different from those given by the moving average crossover systems which keep the trader in the market at all times. Even if some profits are lost by choosing moving averages over trend lines for determining the trend, it should not matter since many "mistakes" will also get avoided.

It must be stressed again that a wholly mechanical system is always better than any system which requires subjectivity because using subjectivity at critical junctures can cause the trader to doubt his conclusions. Traders have many other problems to face in the tense atmosphere of the market and they should at least avoid this problem.

Elliot Wave Theory

In 1939, Ralph Nelson Elliot put forward one of the most complex theories regarding the behavior of stock prices which is now known as Elliot Wave Theory. The theory is based upon what Elliot perceived to be the laws of nature.

Elliot postulated that a bull market rises in five waves while a bear market falls in three waves. The five waves of bull market are said to consist of three up waves, or impulse waves (waves 1, 3 and 5) and two down waves, or corrective waves (waves 2 and 4). A bear market, on the other hand, consists of three waves:

Wave A is the first down wave, followed by a correction, or up wave called Wave B, which is then followed by another longer down wave called Wave C. Furthermore, each of these waves can be subdivided into smaller waves which can be further subdivided into still smaller waves up to the tick level. There are many other rules regarding the size of impulse waves and corrective waves. For a detailed exposition of Elliot Wave Theory, the readers should refer to an excellent book on the subject by Robert C. Beckman.

Although Elliot himself never intended that the theory be used for forecasting, the theory does have a remarkable accuracy in forecasting prices. The practitioners of the theory are said to be handsomely rewarded for their efforts. The major drawback of the theory is that it is very difficult to interpret the waves, and only very rarely do any two analysts agree on the wave count. Even if we are to concede that the theory is useful in spite of its shortcomings, the fact of it being highly subjective cannot be disputed. Furthermore, there are a lot of similarities between traditional technical analysis and Elliot Wave Theory.

For example, let us consider an inverted head and shoulders formation. The rise from the bottom of the head to the neckline can be taken as Elliot's Wave 1 of a bull market. The descent from neckline to the bottom of the right shoulder can be considered as Wave 2 of the bull market. The breakout of neckline from the right shoulder constitutes Wave 3 of the bull market. A contra-trend buy signal at this point is almost invariably received from our system to take advantage of the higher level Wave 3. It is normal for the 13-period moving average line to cross above the 34-period moving average line at the start of Wave 3. As Wave 3 is the longest of the up waves, by the time the Wave 4 correction takes place, the trend is already up even by our definition of the trend. Wave 4 correction will be evidenced by an oversold situation in the lower time frame from where it can be entered by using our pro-trend signal.

Correspondingly, Wave A of a bear market can be entered by using the contra-trend sell signal and Wave C by using the pro-trend sell signal.

It is important to understand that those using the Elliot Wave Theory tend to avoid trading in corrective waves and hence it is rather advantageous that our system is unable to catch down Waves 2 and 4 of the bull markets and up Wave B of the bear market.

There is no guarantee that you will always be long using my system when Wave 3 of a primary bull market starts but then the ensuing corrections of the primary trend will provide you with a sufficient number of pro-trend signals to be able to make useful profits.

Gann Theories

Some of the most difficult theories regarding the behavior of market prices probably come from W. D. Gann, a highly successful US stock and commodity trader. He spent about a decade researching market data and then related them to certain patterns. I must confess that I have not been able to understand these theories at all. Perhaps I don't need to understand them if I just want to make a living from trading. Readers are entitled to form their own opinion after reading more about his theories.

More than his theories, what I found extremely useful was Gann's compilation of 24 rules of trading which he has elaborated in his book, *45 Years in Wall Street*. Of these, the most important rules relate to the dangers of overtrading, and the proper use of money management techniques and stop losses.

It needs to be pointed out once again that every trade contains in itself the possibility of risk as well as reward. Even a user of Gann's methods will never be sure about any particular trade. The only possibility is that the percentage of profitable trades may increase, or the profit per trade may be bigger. Readers are invited to explore these methods further once they gain sufficient experience in stock market trading.

Fibonacci Numbers and Ratios

Fibonacci, a European mathematician, discovered that mathematical relationships exist in natural growth patterns which are seemingly unconnected, and that certain numbers and ratios are more significant than others.

1, 2, 3, 5, 8, 13, 21, 34, 55, 89, 144 and so on are Fibonacci numbers. It will be noticed that in this series of numbers, the sum of any two of the consecutive numbers is the value of the next number in the series.

Furthermore, the ratio between a number and its immediately preceding number is always 1.618, while the ratio between any particular number and the number before the preceding number is always 2.618. The ratio 1.618 is also called the Golden Ratio by mathematicians.

Similarly, the ratios between any one number and next two higher numbers are always, respectively, 0.618 and 0.382.

It has been frequently noticed that Wave 2 correction postulated by Elliot is 0.618 of Wave 1, and that Wave 3 is generally found to be 2.618 of Wave 2. Wave 4 is more likely to end at 0.382 correction level (as measured from Wave 3), and so on.

There is no doubt that the use of these ratios enhances the profitability of any system which a trader may be using, including mine. For a detailed discussion on the subject, the readers should refer to *The Psychology of Technical Analysis* by Tony Plummer. Suffice it to say that those who find themselves unable to use these ratios profitably should not be disheartened since reasonable profits can be made even otherwise.

Momentum Indicators and Divergences

Oscillators, also called momentum indicators, serve mainly two purposes:

1. They indicate oversold and overbought conditions of the market or the stock concerned.
2. They diverge from the price when a reversal may be about to occur.

While defining the parameters of our trading system, it was pointed out that due to confusion regarding the RSI parameters (whether they be 5, 7, 9 or 14) and the levels for oversold and overbought conditions (30, 35 or 40?), we have chosen the 8-period moving average and 21-period moving average crossovers for the same purpose. These numbers (8 and 21) are not only Fibonacci numbers but also correspond very well with intermediate corrections. I don't believe that there is some magic power attached to Fibonacci numbers and a trader is free to experiment in this regard. The reason I prefer these numbers is that they force me to remain disciplined. I have the choice of only a limited set of numbers here, say 3, 5, 8, 13, 21, 34, 55, and so on. Further, the longer term moving average should preferably be between 2 to 3 times the shorter term moving averages and hence we may have combinations of 3 and 8, 5 and 13, 8 and 21, 13 and 34, 21 and 55, and so on. In the trading system being propounded in this book, since we are looking to get into a move in the direction of the higher trend, and a correction is required in the lower time frame to enable a trade entry, the 8 and 21 combination suits our purpose the best. In practice, it approximately corresponds to RSI 9 with oversold and overbought levels set at 40 and 60. However, there is one important difference between the two: since it is a momentum indicator, RSI can sometimes become oversold even during a sideways movement of the market whereas the 8 and 21 moving average combination is dependent upon the actual price fall.

Furthermore, which type of indicator should be used for suggesting oversold and overbought situations also depends upon the manner in which an entry is sought to be made thereafter. Since we are using swing breakouts and breakdowns for entries, we need a significant correction before planning our move. This is easily provided by the 8 and 21 moving average combination.

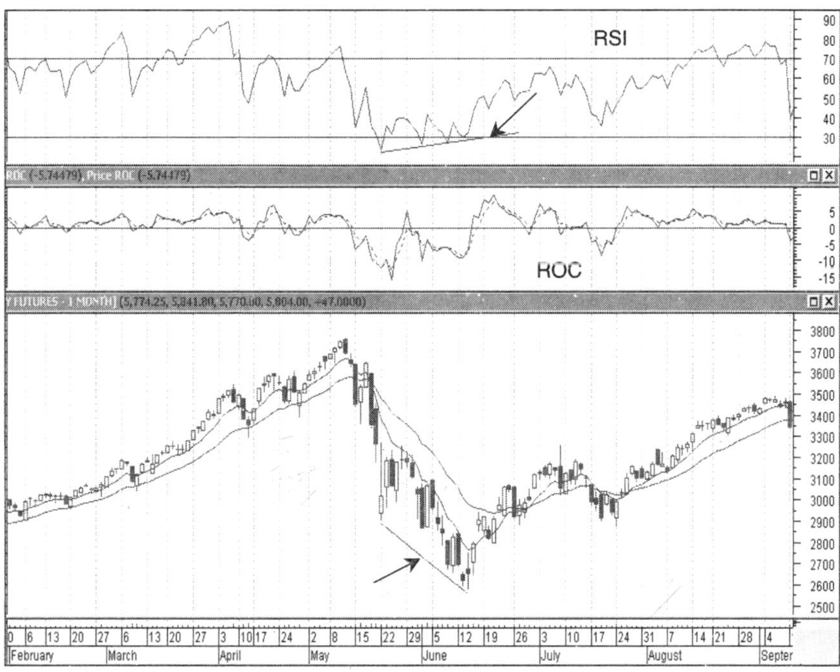

Figure 26.5: **Daily chart of Nifty futures showing positive divergence between price and RSI, at the points highlighted with arrows, where RSI is rising while the price is falling.**

~

The occurrence of non-confirming divergences is the second important role played by momentum indicators. Positive divergences form when both price and indicator first make a simultaneous bottom, then both rise thereafter, and again start falling simultaneously — but while the price makes a new low, the indicator does not. This is better understood by looking at a price chart and momentum indicator simultaneously as in Figure 26.5.

Negative divergences are formed when the opposite occurs, namely when the price makes a higher high but the indicator does not do so (*see* Figure 26.6).

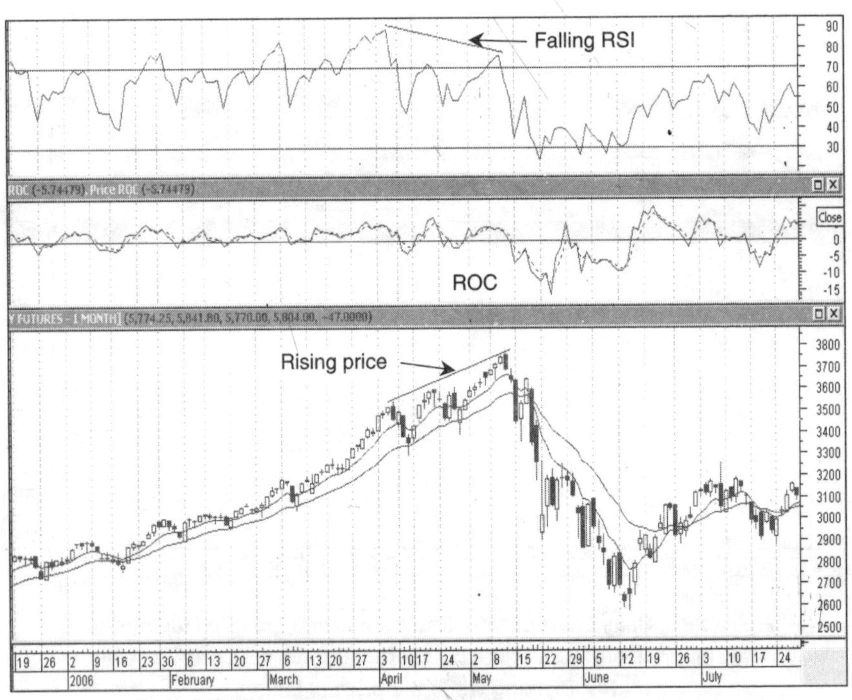

Figure 26.6: **Daily chart of Nifty showing negative divergence, the price is rising even as RSI is falling**

~

Figure 26.6 shows that a negative divergence had become obvious on 10 May on the daily chart. The trader should now be looking for a short sale opportunity.

A trader using our system, however, would be focusing on the hourly charts (intraday charts) for a trade entry. The hourly MACD had gone into sell mode and a swing low was created at 3,690 on 11 May (*see* Figure 26.7). Another swing high was created at 3,748 on the same day. The trader would have gone short when the price subsequently broke the swing low of 3,690, with a stop loss at 3,748.

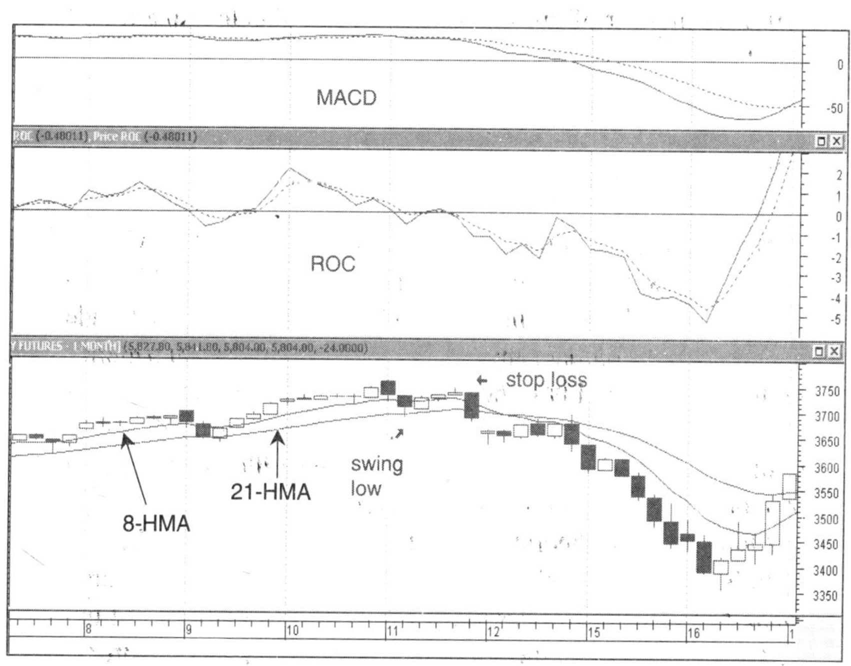

Figure 26.7: **Hourly chart of Nifty futures for a part of the period as shown in Figure 26.6**

The above example demonstrates that our system is capable of taking advantage of divergences without the need for tracking them *via* indicators.

Volume

Is it volume that drives the price or is it the price that drives volume? A chicken or egg kind of situation, more or less!

The price can rise without any accompanying rise in volume, and fall the same way as well. As has been said, however, "the prices need buying to rise but they can fall due to their own weight." A rise in price would normally need interested buyers with money. But that may not necessarily always be true. Price can also rise due to short covering, namely it can rise when bears have to buy in order to square up their short positions. In such cases, however, the rise in volume may not be sustained for long.

A rise in price accompanied by a sustained rise in volume is an indication that a further rise in price is more likely. By then, however, it may be too late to make an entry. **One of the most important secrets of stock markets is that when a bull market is confirmed by all indicators, it may actually be about to end; or, at least, temporarily consolidate.**

If a trader wants to take a position only after volume has confirmed the price rise, then he should wait for a correction and take his position during the correction, namely during a quiet period when volumes are relatively low and prices are falling from their most recent highs.

But what if a correction does not take place?

Well, if you are making your first trade and happen to miss the opportunity, there may still be time but what about the trader who was trading the previous signals and has also accumulated losses from his previous trades? The chance of entering a steep bull run may be taken away from him if there is no correction this time.

In Figure 26.8, we can see that the long trade should have been entered on 6 September 2010 when the previous swing high of 5,543 (Line 1 in Figure 26.8) was broken on the up side. You may recall that this trade was earlier been discussed in Chapter 17. There it was done without taking volume into consideration. It is obvious from the volume panel that the volume was low until 14 September, after which it rose significantly and the trader using volume as a confirmatory signal would have gone

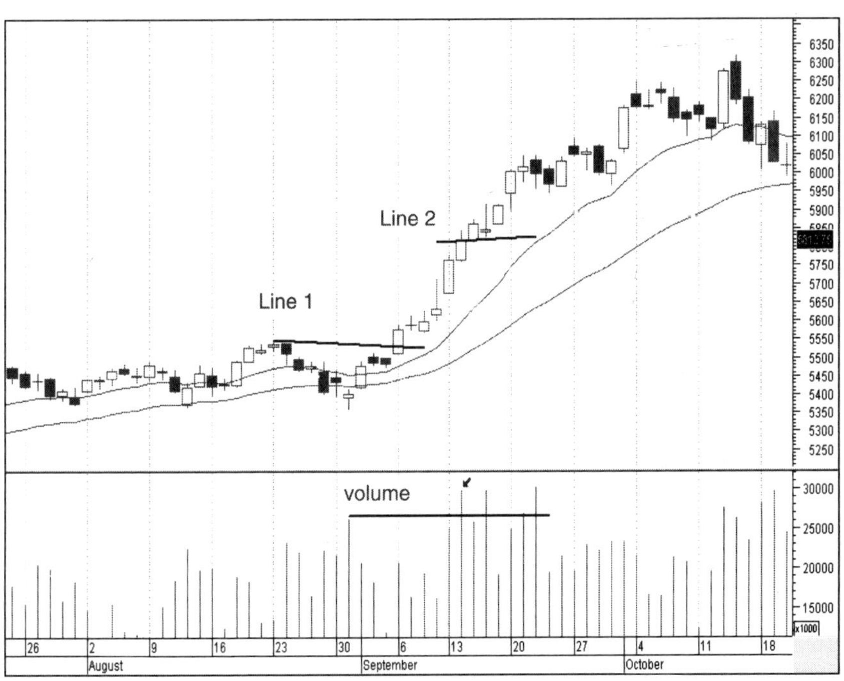

Figure 26.8: **Daily chart of Nifty futures showing volume in the lower panel in histogram format**

~

long at the closing of that day, namely at 5,817 (Line 2 in Figure 26.8). This trade was finally exited at 6,114. Furthermore, there would have been no opportunity to enter a long position had the trader waited for a correction, because there was none.

The stop loss in this trade would have to be placed at the swing low of 5,356, and using the percentage risk method of position sizing outlined in our trading system, the trader, ignoring volume, would have purchased 267 Nifty units whereas the trader using volume for confirmation would have purchased only 97 units, on a risk of ₹50,000. The former trade would have made ₹1,52,000 whereas the latter trade would have made only ₹29,000.

Those who are interested in somehow incorporating volume into their overall strategy should do further research and draw their own conclusions. So far as I am concerned, I am perfectly happy to ignore volume in my trading. The reason is not that it may not be useful but that I need to keep my system as simple as possible.

Open Interest

Open interest is a term which is applicable only to the futures and options markets. It is defined as the total number of contracts which are outstanding at the end of a trading day.

- If a market is rising along with a rising open interest, the trend is said to be healthy, namely further rises are more likely.
- If a market is rising but the open interest is falling, the trend is said to be suspect, namely the up move may be coming to an end.

The same logic, in reverse, can be applied to bear markets.

Like in the case of volume, I have not found open interest to be of much use in my trading system.

One of the most significant pitfalls of technical analysis is that there are too many indicators serving the same purpose. It is for a trader to decide which ones to use and which to discard. For example, if the trend in the weekly time frame is up, namely the 13WMA line is above the 34WMA line, then the point to remember is that at some time in the past the trend was down. It could have turned up only when actual buying took place. From time to time, the uptrend will face minor corrections. During corrections, the open interest may or may not fall. If there is a substantial reduction in open interest, then it is unlikely that price will rise any further and give a buy signal. If the fall in open interest is minor, then there are two possibilities — either accumulation, or distribution, is in progress. It is almost impossible to decide what is happening in real time, i.e. when you do not have thc benefit of hindsight. In any case, all indicators have their own failure and success rates. Further, these rates are also dependent upon the trader's interpretation of an indicator.

If you have found a reliable way of using open interest, then use it by all mean, but I would be surprised if you can find a way of using more than five indicators at one time.

> What traders should remember at all times is that there is no Holy Grail. It is all about risk and money management. You can even make money with an inferior system if you manage your risk well or else the best system in the world will not be of any use to you.

Put Call Ratio (PCR)

Put call ratio is the ratio of outstanding put options divided by outstanding call options.

This ratio is a little more transparent as compared to open interest in the sense that open interest does not inform us whether more long positions or more short positions are being built up, but the put call ratio is straight forward. If the ratio is more than one, then obviously there are more puts outstanding than calls, and hence traders are expecting the market to fall, and *vice versa*.

The ratio is used more as a contrary indicator. If more people are bearish, then rather than falling the market is more likely to rise since most people are wrong in their estimation of future prices. PCR, however, is a rather long term predictor of where the prices may be headed and can't really be effectively used with our trading system.

~

Part 4

~

Trading in Real Life

27

~

Technical Analysis Software

Plenty of technical analysis software is now available which makes a trader's task easier. Personally, I use Metastock. The software and data services may cost a minimum of ₹5,000 per year but these prices are continuously reducing.

The Metastock software can be installed on any modern computer and does not require much computing power. The end of day data can be downloaded every day after 3.30P.M., while hourly data can be downloaded at the end of each hour.

You will also need to customize the software screen. If you plan to use the method proposed in this book, you should arrange the screen in the following manner:

- Price chart in the form of candlesticks (or bars) at the bottom.
- Price ROC of 5 days just above the price chart (in blue color).
- A 3-period moving average of ROC in the form of blue dotted line.
- MACD at the top (in red color).

Now plot the following exponential moving averages on the price chart:

- 8-period: Blue (solid).
- 21-period: Red (solid).
- 13-period: Blue (dotted).
- 34-period: Red (dotted).

This is only indicative and you can make changes in the settings as you grow more experienced with the software.

~

28

~

Trading Protocol

Pre-Trade Check

1. Switch the customized chart to weekly time frame and note whether the 13WMA line is above or below the 34WMA line.
2. Change the time frame to daily and note whether the 8DMA line is above or below the 21DMA line.
3. Also note whether daily MACD is in buy mode or sell mode. MACD is considered in buy mode when the solid line is above the dotted line — and *vice versa*.

Trade Entry

Use the following rules to decide entry:

When 13WMA is above 34WMA:

Scenario 1

Wait for the 8DMA line to go below the 21DMA line and thereafter buy on the swing breakout.

This trading signal is to be taken irrespective of whether the daily MACD is in the buy mode or the sell mode.

Full risk is to be taken.

Scenario 2

If the daily MACD goes into sell mode when the 8DMA line is above the 21 DMA line, short sell on swing breakdown. Half of the usual risk should be taken.

When this occurs, you may also be having a long position as per Scenario 1. If this be the case, then the breakdown of a swing after the daily MACD goes into a sell mode would require both exiting the long position — and going short simultaneously.

Scenario 3

You are holding a short position as per Scenario 2 above and a swing breakout occurs on the upside. If the price had moved down after the establishment of short position, then the initial stop loss may also get shifted downwards. **In such a case, hitting of the stop loss entails the exiting it short position also automatically going long.**

If the stop loss is hit while the 8DMA line is still above the 21DMA line, then half the usual risk is taken in going long.

If the 8DMA line has gone below the 21DMA line, then full risk is taken as per Scenario 1.

When 13WMA is Below 34WMA:

Scenario 1

Wait for the 8DMA line to go above the 21DMA line and thereafter sell on a swing breakdown. This signal is to be taken irrespective of whether the daily MACD is in buy or sell mode.

This is a full risk trade.

Scenario 2

If the daily MACD goes into buy mode when the 8DMA line is below the 21 DMA line, go long on swing breakout. Half of the usual risk is to be taken.

When this occurs, you may also be having a short position as per Scenario 1. If this be the case, then the breakout of a swing after the daily MACD goes into a buy mode would require both exiting the short position — and going long simultaneously.

Scenario 3

Now let's suppose a long position as per Scenario 2 above already exists and a swing breakdown occurs on the downside. If the price had moved up after the initiation of the long position, then the initial stop loss may get shifted upward. In that case, the hitting of stop loss in the long position automatically requires going short.

If the stop loss is hit while the 8DMA line is still below the 21DMA line, then half the usual risk is taken when going short.

If, on the other hand, the 8DMA line has gone above the 21DMA line then full risk is taken as per Scenario 1.

Exits

All positions, whether long or short, must be exited when a swing break occurs in the opposite direction.

Let's consider this in a little more detail.

Once a long position is created, an initial stop loss is placed immediately below the bottom of the most recent swing. The actual stop loss entered in the trading terminal will be slightly different from the estimated stop loss as explained in Chapter 9.

If the price subsequently rises, then the stop loss is shifted upward upon the formation of a new swing. In other words, let's suppose that an upswing is created while going long (let us call it swing A), followed by a downswing (let us call this Swing B) followed by another upswing (let us call Swing C). Once Swing C is created, the stop loss should be moved up to below the bottom of Swing B. This is our trailing stop loss and it can be raised further in similar manner if there is any further rise in price. The trade will be exited once the latest trailing stop loss — or the initial stop loss in case it hasn't been shifted up — is hit, whichever happens first.

The reverse is true for short positions as explained below.

Once a short position is created, an initial stop loss is placed immediately above the top of the most recent swing. If the price subsequently falls, then the stop loss is shifted downward on the formation of a new swing. In other words, let's suppose that while going short, a downswing is created (let us call it swing A), followed by an upswing (let us call it Swing B) followed by another downswing (let us call this Swing C). Once Swing C is created, the stop loss should be moved up to above the top of Swing B. This is our trailing stop loss and it can be lowered further in similar manner if there is any further fall in price.

The trade will be exited once the latest trailing stop loss — or the initial stop loss in case it hadn't been shifted down — is hit, whichever happens first.

~

29

~

Nifty *versus* Sensex

Some investors get confused regarding the superiority of one index over the other. While Nifty is the broad market index of the National Stock Exchange (NSE) and consists of 50 large capitalization stocks from diverse sectors of the economy, Sensex is similarly a broad based index of 30 stocks and is owned by the Bombay Stock Exchange (BSE).

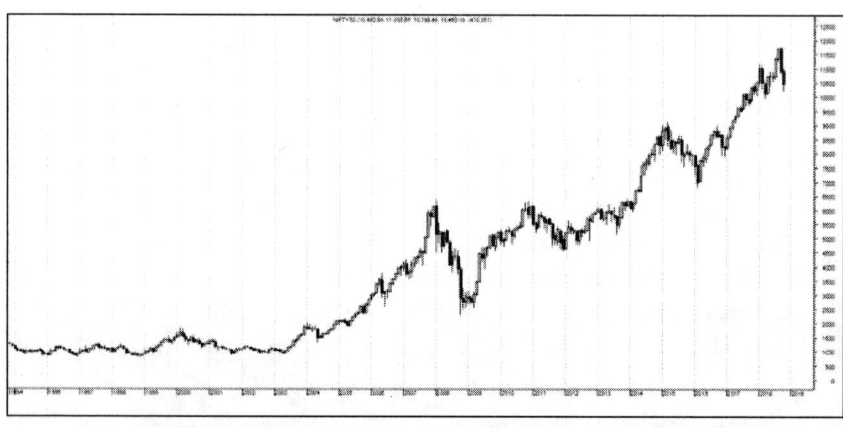

Figure 29.1: **Monthly chart of Nifty since its inception in 1994**

~

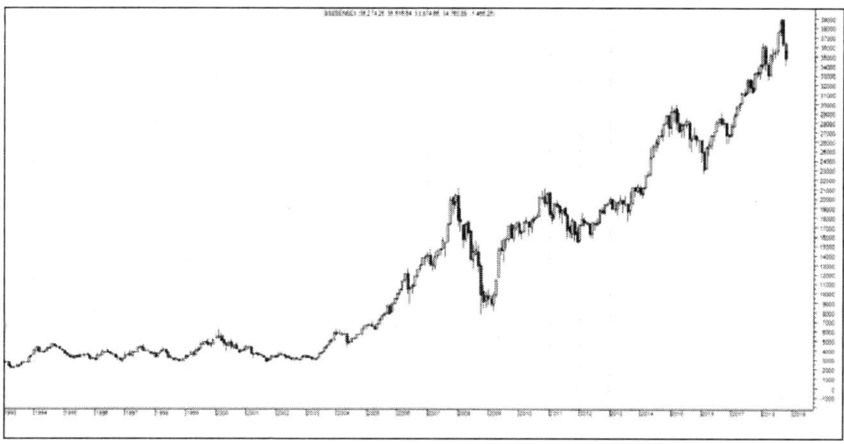

Figure 29.2: **Monthly chart of Sensex for the same period, namely 1994-2018**

~

Table 29.1 highlights the important statistics about these two indices:

Table 29.1

Date	*Nifty*	*Sensex*
01/01/1995	1,182	3,927
05/10/2018	10,316	34,377
Return	**773%**	**775%**

Over a period of 23 years, Sensex returned 2% more than Nifty, a difference of only 0.09% per annum over such a long period. Even this difference may be more due to chance than any formula or the composition of the indices.

Futures trading does not exist in Sensex, which is only a tracking device. If you want to trade in index futures, then Nifty futures is the only available choice. You may also trade in Bank Nifty futures which has quite good liquidity. A limited number of individual stock futures are also available on the NSE platform but none are available on the BSE platform.

References and Further Reading

— Ashley, Gerald: *Trading Financial Biases and Behaviour.*

— Beckman, Robert C.: *Elliot Wave Explained* (Vision Books, Delhi).

— Bernstein, Jake: *Market Masters* (Vision Books, Delhi).

— Bernstein, Jake: *Profits in the Futures Markets* (Vision Books, Delhi).

— Case, Cynthia: *Trading With the Odds.*

— Edwards, Robert and Maggie, John: *Technical Analysis of Stock Trends* (Vision Books, Delhi).

— Elder, Alexander: *Trading for a Living.*

— Eng, William F.: *The Technical Analysis of Stocks, Options & Futures* (Vision Books, Delhi).

— Fosback, Norman G.: *Stock Market Logic* (Vision Books, Delhi).

— Gann, W. D.: 45 *Years in Wall Street.*

— Kiyosaki, Robert: *Rich Dad, Poor Dad.*

— O'Shaughnessy, *What Works on Wall Street (*Mcgraw Hill).

— Plummer, Tony: *The Psychology of Technical Analysis* (Vision Books, Delhi).

— Pring, Martin J.: *Martin Pring on Market Momentum* (Vision — Books, Delhi).

— Tharp, Van K.: *Trade Your Way to Financial Freedom.*